Frommer's

Cornwall
day BY day
1st Edition

by Sue Viccars

WILEY

A John Wiley and Sons, Ltd, Publication

Contents

Copyright © 2010 John Wiley & Sons Ltd, The Atrium, Southern Gate,
Chichester, West Sussex PO19 8SQ, England
Telephone (+44) 1243 779777
Email (for orders and customer service enquiries): cs-books@wiley.co.uk.
Visit our Home Page on www.wiley.com

UK Publisher: Sally Smith
Production Manager: Daniel Mersey
Commissioning Editor: Mark Henshall
Development Editor: Lindsay Hunt
Content Editor: Erica Peters
Photo Research: David Cottingham
Cartography: Jeremy Norton

Wiley also publishes its books in a variety of electronic formats. Some
content that appears in print may not be available in electronic books.

British Library Cataloguing in Publication Data
A catalogue record for this book is available from the British Library

ISBN: 978-0-470-72100-1

Typeset by Wiley Indianapolis Composition Services
Printed and bound in China by RR Donnelley

5   4   3   2   1

A Note from the Editorial Director

Organizing your time. That's what this guide is all about.

Other guides give you long lists of things to see and do and then expect you to fit the pieces together. The Day by Day guides are different. These guides tell you the best of everything, and then they show you how to see it *in the smartest, most time-efficient way*. Our authors have designed detailed itineraries organized by time, neighborhood, or special interest. And each tour comes with a bulleted map that takes you from stop to stop.

Hoping to relax in the sunshine at Nanjizal, one of Cornwall's most beautiful beaches, eat real ice cream at Roskillys or walk to the romantic St Michael's Mount? Planning to enter a world of medieval Arthurian legends at Tintagel Island or watch seals basking on the Western Rocks of the Isles of Scilly? Whatever your interest or schedule, the Day by Days give you the smartest routes to follow. Not only do we take you to the top attractions, hotels, and restaurants, but we also help you access those special moments that locals get to experience—those "finds" that turn tourists into travelers.

The Day by Days are also your top choice if you're looking for one complete guide for all your travel needs. The best hotels and restaurants for every budget, the greatest shopping values, the wildest nightlife—it's all here.

Why should you trust our judgment? Because our authors personally visit each place they write about. They're an independent lot who say what they think and would never include places they wouldn't recommend to their best friends. They're also open to suggestions from readers. If you'd like to contact them, please send your comments our way at feedback@frommers.com, and we'll pass them on.

Enjoy your Day by Day guide—the most helpful travel companion you can buy. And have the trip of a lifetime.

Warm regards,

Kelly Regan

Kelly Regan, Editorial Director
Frommer's Travel Guides

About the Author

Sue Viccars has been exploring Cornwall for a long, long time. When she was a child she spent family holidays on a farm near Mevagissey, and has memories of riding the farm pony, days on the beach at Caerhays on the south coast and dodging the surf at Crantock on the north. Later she rented a cottage at Constantine Bay near Padstow; odd weekends in Polruan, Falmouth, Zennor and Penzance followed, and soon she began to explore the South West Coast Path along the county's cliffs – and Bodmin Moor – on foot. With her sons she has cycled the Camel Trail and Portreath Tramroad, holidayed in Port Isaac, and camped on St Martin's and Bryher in the Isles of Scilly. Work for a number of publishers has over the last few years involved research in all aspects of what makes Cornwall special: great walks, excellent places to eat, a huge range of places to stay, fascinating history and archaeology, flora and fauna — and, of course, the county's exceptionally beautiful coastline.

This book details a number of tours which will introduce the reader to the best of what Cornwall has to offer, and will highlight why it is the best holiday destination in the UK. It is little wonder that once discovered this most southwesterly outpost of the UK draws people back again and again. . . .

Acknowledgements

It would be impossible to list everyone I've talked to while researching this book, so I'd just like to thank all those accommodation providers who showed me round, the restaurant and café owners who answered endless questions, and the owners of many of Cornwall's best attractions who admitted me without charge. I would also like to thank my brother David who, although usually based in Bangkok, chose to spend a couple of weeks with me in the book's early stages. He now knows more about Cornwall's mining heritage sites than he ever thought possible, and has an intimate knowledge of St Ives! His company (and generosity) was very much appreciated, and our time together was a real treat. Yet again Jane provided stalwart support in the form of food, wine and a comfortable bed while I researched Truro and Falmouth, and Julia provided the same while exploring the Helford region. And finally my thanks go to Stu, as ever, for his patient support during both the research and writing of this book, and for putting up with (at times incessant) discussions about it. His support is much more important than he realises!

Dedication

For Nick and Joffy

An Additional Note

Please be advised that travel information is subject to change at any time—and this is especially true of prices. We therefore suggest that you write or call ahead for confirmation when making your travel plans. The authors, editors, and publisher cannot be held responsible for the experiences of readers while travelling. Your safety is important to us, however, so we encourage you to stay alert and be aware of your surroundings.

Star Ratings, Icons & Abbreviations

Every hotel, restaurant, and attraction listing in this guide has been ranked for quality, value, service, amenities, and special features using a **star-rating system.** Hotels, restaurants, attractions, shopping, and nightlife are rated on a scale of zero stars (recommended) to three stars (exceptional). In addition to the star-rating system, we also use a **kids icon** to point out the best bets for families. Within each tour, we recommend cafes, bars, or restaurants where you can take a break. Each of these stops appears in a shaded box marked with a coffee-cup-shaped bullet ☕.

The following **abbreviations** are used for credit cards:

AE	American Express	DISC	Discover	V	Visa
DC	Diners Club	MC	MasterCard		

Travel Resources at Frommers.com

Frommer's travel resources don't end with this guide. Frommer's website, **www.frommers.com,** has travel information on more than 4,000 destinations. We update features regularly, giving you access to the most current trip-planning information and the best airfare, lodging, and car-rental bargains. You can also listen to podcasts, connect with other Frommers.com members through our active-reader forums, share your travel photos, read blogs from guidebook editors and fellow travellers, and much more.

How to Contact Us

In researching this book, we discovered many wonderful places—hotels, restaurants, shops, and more. We're sure you'll find others. Please tell us about them, so we can share the information with your fellow travellers in upcoming editions. If you were disappointed with a recommendation, we'd love to know that, too. Please write to:

Frommer's Cornwall Day by Day, 1st Edition
Wiley Publishing, Inc. • 111 River St. • Hoboken, NJ 07030-5774

20 Favourite
Moments

20 Favourite **Moments**

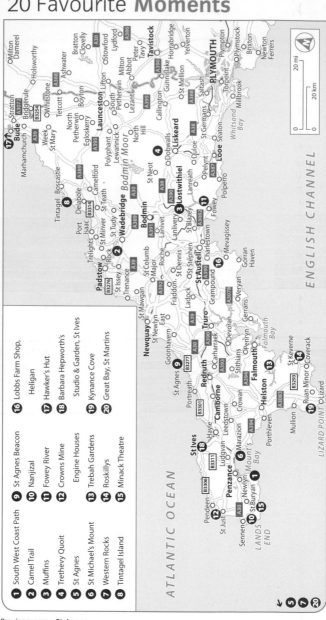

1 South West Coast Path
2 Camel Trail
3 Muffins
4 Trethevy Quoit
5 St Agnes
6 St Michael's Mount
7 Western Rocks
8 Tintagel Island
9 St Agnes Beacon
10 Nanjizal
11 Fowey River
12 Crowns Mine
13 Trebah Gardens
14 Roskillys
15 Minack Theatre
16 Lobbs Farm Shop, Heligan
17 Hawker's Hut
18 Barbara Hepworth's Studio & Garden, St Ives
19 Kynance Cove
20 Great Bay, St Martins

Previous page: St Agnes.

Selecting just 20 'Favourite Moments' in a county as diverse as Cornwall is a tantalising challenge. Discovering Cornwall's mining heritage on the cliffs of West Penwith, sampling delicious Cornish fare in historic Lostwithiel, or simply drinking in the stunning views from the top of St Agnes Beacon are just a few unforgettable memories that the UK's most southwesterly county has to offer.

① **Enjoying the scent of dog violets and wild daffodils** on the South West Coast Path between Lamorna and Mousehole in spring. *See p 130.*

② **Feeling the wind in your hair as you cycle along the Camel Trail** from Wadebridge to Padstow for fish 'n' chips at Rick Stein's takeaway. *See p 85.*

③ **Tucking into a 'taster plate' of Cornish meats,** fish, relishes and breads at Muffins in Lostwithiel. *See p 119.*

④ **Marvelling at the prowess of prehistoric megalithic builders** at Trethevy Quoit on Bodmin Moor. *See p 55,* **⑬**.

⑤ **Circuiting St Agnes, the UK's most southwesterly island,** and picking up an ice cream from Troy Town Farm on the way. *See p 168.*

⑥ **Approaching St Michael's Mount on foot or by boat:** a fortified priory and castle romantically

Trethevy Quoit, Bodmin Moor.

set on a rocky outcrop, cut off at high tide. *See p 57,* **①**.

⑦ **Watching seals basking on the Western Rocks** of the Isles of Scilly from a small boat. *See p 168,* **㉚**.

⑧ **Scaling the 100 or so steep, uneven steps at Tintagel Island,** and stepping back to a world of medieval Arthurian legends. *See p 64,* **⑭**.

Mousehole harbour, southwest Cornwall.

9 **Standing on top of St Agnes Beacon near Newquay** and enjoying the breathtaking panoramic 360° view. *See p 81.*

10 **Relaxing in the sunshine at Nanjizal,** near Lands End, one of Cornwall's most beautiful beaches—only accessible on foot. *See p 68.*

11 **Exploring the sheltered and secluded creeks of the Fowey River,** and visiting the ancient church at St Winnow. *See p 149.*

12 **Admiring the view over the old Crowns Mine Engine Houses** on the cliffs at Botallack on a summer's evening. *See p 24,* **8** .

13 **Weaving your way through subtropical trees and shrubs** along narrow paths and steps at Trebah Gardens on the Helford river. *See p 30,* **7** .

14 **Eating real Cornish ice cream** at Roskillys on the Lizard, Callestick at Penhallow or Moomaid from the Wayside Museum at Zennor. *See p 41.*

15 **Experiencing an open-air theatrical performance** at the Minack Theatre, carved out of the cliffs at Porthcurno. *See p 35,* **2** .

Crowns Mine, Botallack, West Penwith.

The beach at Nanjizal, southwest Cornwall.

16 **Buying local meat, cheese, fruit and veg from Lobbs Farm Shop, Heligan**—or visiting any of Cornwall's flourishing farmers markets—and knowing that you're helping the Cornish economy. *See p 175.*

17 **Squeezing into Hawker's Hut to escape the rain,** and then treating yourself to the best cream tea in Cornwall at the Rectory Farm Tea Room in Morwenstow. *See p 98.*

18 **Visiting Barbara Hepworth's Studio & Garden** in St Ives, left just as it was when she lived and worked here. *See p 47.*

19 **Sitting on the cliffs overlooking Kynance Cove,** eating a pasty bought from Ann's Pasty Shop in Lizard village. *See p 68.*

20 **Strolling along the sands of Great Bay on St Martins,** one of the most beautiful beaches on the Isles of Scilly, and exploring White Island at low tide. *See p 68.* ●

Strategies for Seeing **Cornwall**

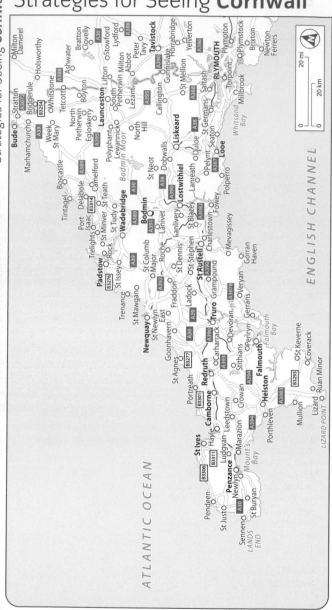

Previous page: The beach at Porthcurno.

A glance at any map shows that Cornwall isn't a very large county—it's much smaller than neighbouring Devon, for example. It measures just 1,375 sq miles (3,563 sq km) in area, and 80 miles (129 km) from the Devon border at the River Tamar to Lands End. Therefore, you might think it would be easy to explore in a day or so; after all, public transport links between larger towns are fairly frequent. But train services away from the main Paddington–Penzance line are very limited and buses to small villages sporadic. If you want to explore Cornwall in depth within a limited time-frame, the only practical way of getting around is by car.

Rule #1: Time your holiday

The tourist season in Cornwall is no longer restricted to the traditional Easter and summer holidays: short breaks are popular all year round. That said, Cornwall's resident population of 500,000 or so still increases by 50% during the main school holidays: Easter, May half-term and from mid-July to early September. If you have children there's no way round this problem; if you don't, it's best to avoid these periods.

Rule #2: Allow enough time to get around

The two main access roads leading into Cornwall are the A30 running over Bodmin Moor to Penzance, and the A38 from Plymouth in Devon, which meets the A30 at Bodmin. In winter, most roads will be relatively quiet, but at weekends in high season traffic can be very heavy on the main holiday routes. Many accommodation bookings run from Friday or Saturday, and on those days many holidaymakers travel to and from Cornwall. Allow plenty of time for your journey; expect delays; travel at night if feasible; and take food and drink for the trip. If at all possible, find accommodation that doesn't have a Friday or Saturday changeover.

Rule #3: Consider a multi-centre holiday

If you're planning to spend a week on the beach a one-centre holiday is fine, but if you're interested in delving into the county's history, archaeology, landscape and so on, you may want to move around. Note, however, that it can be difficult to make 1-night accommodation bookings in high season (from Easter to end of September). Cornwall can be split into four regions: southeast (p 149), Bodmin Moor and the north coast (p 143), central (including the Roseland and Lizard Peninsulas, p 155) and the far southwest — including the Isles of Scilly (p 163). Each area has a distinct character and different appeal (see Chapter 6).

Tintagel Island, north Cornwall.

View across Crooklets on a rough day.

Cornwall's large estuaries make exploring Cornwall more time-consuming than you might expect, and ferries can be surprisingly expensive.

Rule #4: Make use of local transport deals

Unless you're staying in a very remote area, it's worth asking about local transport facilities. You can't reach everywhere in Cornwall by public transport, but you can save motoring costs by using discount parking deals or park-and-ride schemes. Some district councils offer week-long parking tickets (typically costing around £30), which can be used in any of their car parks, otherwise standard municipal parking charges can add up fast: many car parks charge for 24 hours, 7 days a week, and tariffs range from £1 per hour to £6–8 for 3 hours at some privately-owned car parks. Visit local Tourist Information Centres for information.

In addition, National Trust (NT) members can save money on parking and entrance charges. English Heritage, The Royal Horticultural Society (RHS) and The Royal Society for the Protection of Birds (RSPB) cards are also good value. Lastly, take binoculars if you're keen on birds, and perhaps specialist guides for identifying flora and fauna.

Rule #5: Brush up your driving and navigation skills

You need to get off the main roads to get the most out of a visit to Cornwall. Many of the best beaches, more picturesque villages and interesting historic houses lie off major routes. Remember, though, that remote parts of Cornwall may have patchy mobile phone coverage, and sat-nav systems may not be 100% reliable either. Get hold of up-to-date Ordnance Survey Explorer (OS) or Landranger maps for the areas you want to visit, and learn how to use them accurately and efficiently (www.ordnancesurvey.co.uk/leisure). Many of Cornwall's minor roads are single track, and you will inevitably meet oncoming vehicles from time to time: brush up on your reversing skills. Many of the tours recommended in this book involve negotiating narrow country lanes. ●

The Best of Cornwall
in a Long Weekend

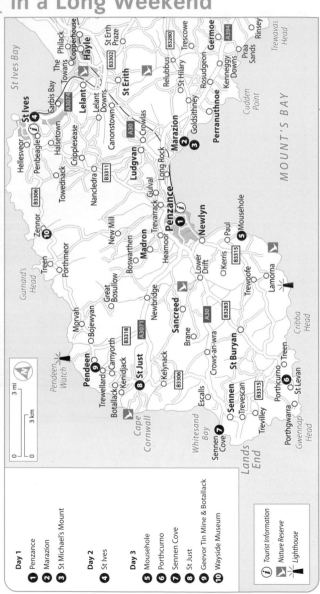

Day 1
1. Penzance
2. Marazion
3. St Michael's Mount

Day 2
4. St Ives

Day 3
5. Mousehole
6. Porthcurno
7. Sennen Cove
8. St Just
9. Geevor Tin Mine & Botallack
10. Wayside Museum

i Tourist Information
Nature Reserve
Lighthouse

Previous page: Boats at Sennen Cove.

If you have only 2 or 3 days in Cornwall, prioritise your interests carefully, for example, history, archaeology, walking, the arts. For a varied 'taster pack' of what Cornwall has to offer, head for West Penwith. This is the area closest to Lands End, that part of Cornwall most physically and emotionally distant from the rest of England. It's a smallish area (only 7 miles/11¼km) across the narrow 'neck' between St Ives Bay and Marazion), but once off the main roads, lanes are narrow and twisting, and can't be tackled quickly. Base yourself in Penzance, Penwith's main town, and in 3 days you'll get a real feel of what makes Cornwall 'tick'.

Travel Tip

For more information on sights, recommended accommodation and places to eat, see the individual sections on Penzance and St Ives in Chapter 5, and the 'Ancient Cornwall' and 'Cornwall's Arts & Crafts' tours in Chapter 3.

Day One

Spend the morning in **1 Penzance.** Visit the Penlee House Gallery & Museum and historic Chapel Street, said to be the most haunted street in Britain (p 129, **2**). In the afternoon drive 3½ miles (5½km) east along Mount's Bay to **2 Marazion** (p 48, **12**) and take a trip to **3 St Michael's Mount** (p 57, **1**).

Day Two

Take the train from Penzance to **4 St Ives** (p 46, **10**); the Cornwall Branch Line Ranger ticket (adult 4 gives unlimited travel for a day. GroupSave enables four people to travel for the price of two).

Day Three

Drive west to **5 Mousehole** and **6 Porthcurno**, and then to mainland Britain's most southwesterly village, **7 Sennen Cove** (16 miles/ 26km). Drive north via **8 St Just** to **9 Geevor Tin Mine & Botallack** (p 23, **6**). Spend the afternoon at the **10 Wayside Museum** in Zennor (p 54, **10**).

Walking the South West Coast Path

If you're reasonably fit, you can walk the distance from St Ives to Penzance in three fairly strenuous days: St Ives to Pendeen (13½ miles/22km), Pendeen to Porthcurno (16 miles/26km) and Porthcurno to Penzance (11¼ miles/18km). It's a tough, beautiful route, suitable only for experienced walkers; some parts have no facilities. Some accommodation-providers operate a luggage transfer service, but you need to book ahead. See www.swcp.org.uk/luggage-transfers-south-west.html for details (costs are typically around £13 for two bags). Buses and trains connect Penzance with St Ives (see Chapter 5 and Savvy Traveller).

Cornwall **in One Week**

The Best Full-Day Tours

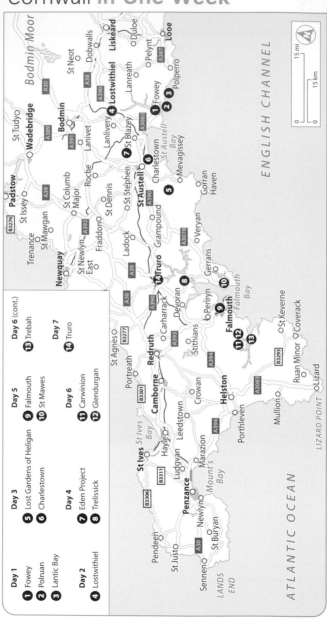

Day 1
1. Fowey
2. Polruan
3. Lantic Bay

Day 2
4. Lostwithiel

Day 3
5. Lost Gardens of Heligan
6. Charlestown

Day 4
7. Eden Project
8. Trelissick

Day 5
9. Falmouth
10. St Mawes

Day 6
11. Carwinion
12. Glendurgan

Day 6 (cont.)
13. Trebah

Day 7
14. Truro

Making the most of 7 days in Cornwall is best done by arranging a two-centre holiday. You won't manage to visit every corner of the county, but if you spend your first few nights in Fowey and the rest in Falmouth (both on the south coast) you'll be able to see a range of different towns and visit some of Cornwall's best historic houses, castles and gardens, including the Eden Project. You should also have time for an afternoon on the beach or a boat trip from Falmouth upriver to Truro, Cornwall's county town.

Travel Tip

For more information on sights, recommended accommodation and places to eat, see the individual sections on Fowey, Lostwithiel and Truro in Chapter 5, parts of the 'Special Interest Tours' in Chapter 3 and parts of the 'Regional Tours' in Chapter 6.

Day One

Spend the morning in **1 Fowey,** and visit St Catherine's Castle. Take the ferry to **2 Polruan** to see the 14th-century blockhouse; have a bite to eat at the Lugger Inn on the quay. A 1½-mile (2½km) walk along the South West South West Coast Path takes you to **3 Lantic Bay** (p 67).

Day Two

Drive to ancient **4 Lostwithiel** (6¼ miles/10km); visit Restormel Castle and have lunch at Muffins (p 119). Spend the afternoon at stately Lanhydrock House (p 60, **8**).

Day Three

Drive west to explore the **5 Lost Gardens of Heligan** (14 miles/ 22½km) (p 27, **1**), stopping off en route for a coffee at the atmospheric Georgian port of **6 Charlestown** (p 106, **9**).

Day Four

Spend the whole morning at the **7 Eden Project** (6 miles/9½km) (p 40, **12**); go early to beat the queues in peak holiday times, and

have lunch there before setting off for Falmouth. You can take the main A390 through Truro, or go via the Roseland Peninsula and the King Harry Ferry (p 63). If you have time, call in at **8 Trellissick** (p 28, **4**) (29 miles/47km).

Day Five

A day in **9 Falmouth:** visit the Maritime Museum in the morning, and then take the ferry across the Carrick Roads to picturesque **10 St Mawes** and its castle (p 59, **4**).

Day Six

A day to explore the lovely gardens on the Helford river: **11 Carwinion** (p 29, **5**), **12 Glendurgan** (p 29, **6**) and **13 Trebah** (p 30, **7**) (4¼ miles/6¾km).

Day Seven

Go on a river trip up the Fal to **14 Truro** with Enterprise Boats (p 138, **11**); visit the cathedral and Royal Cornwall Museum, allowing time for a bit of shopping in Lemon Street Market.

Truro Cathedral.

Cornwall **in Two Weeks**

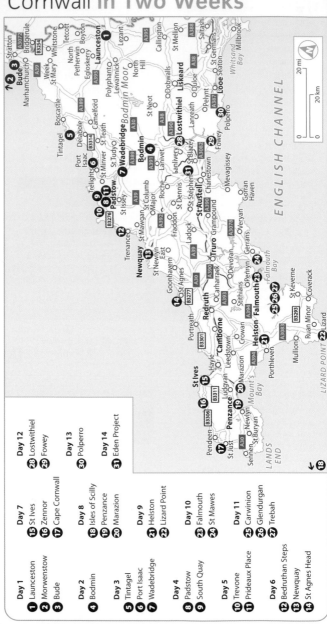

Day 1
1. Launceston
2. Morwenstow
3. Bude

Day 2
4. Bodmin

Day 3
5. Tintagel
6. Port Isaac
7. Wadebridge

Day 4
8. Padstow
9. South Quay

Day 5
10. Trevone
11. Prideaux Place

Day 6
12. Bedruthan Steps
13. Newquay
14. St Agnes Head

Day 7
15. St Ives
16. Zennor
17. Cape Cornwall

Day 8
18. Isles of Scilly
19. Penzance
20. Marazion

Day 9
21. Helston
22. Lizard Point

Day 10
23. Falmouth
24. St Mawes

Day 11
25. Carwinion
26. Glendurgan
27. Trebah

Day 12
28. Lostwithiel
29. Fowey

Day 13
30. Polperro

Day 14
31. Eden Project

If you're lucky enough to have 2 weeks to spend in Cornwall, you need to decide whether to 'hotel-hop' every 2 or 3 nights if you have that flexibility, or base yourself in one place for the first week and a different place for the second. Chapter 5 on the 'Best Towns' gives some suggestions for hotel, guesthouse and B&B accommodation, but if you're planning full-week stays you may want to consider renting self-catering accommodation, which nearly always works out cheaper (p 25). The recommended tour below allows for a 2-night stay at each destination.

Travel Tip

For more information on sights, recommended accommodation and places to eat, see the individual town entries in Chapter 5, parts of the 'Special Interest Tours' in Chapter 3 and parts of the 'Regional Tours' in Chapter 6.

Morwenstow church from the South West Coast Path.

Day One

Start in ❶ **Launceston** (p 109): visit the castle, drive to ❷ **Morwenstow** on the north coast for lunch (26 miles/42km) (p 98) and then pop into ❸ **Bude** on the way home.

Day Two

Take the A30 to ❹ **Bodmin** (22½ miles/36km) (p 93); follow the first half of the Bodmin Moor and North Coast Tour (p 113).

Day Three

Drive west on the A395; pick up signs for ❺ **Tintagel** (19½ miles/31¼km) (p 64, ⓮), take the coast road via ❻ **Port Isaac** to ❼ **Wadebridge** (p 126, ⓫) and then to Padstow (p 125).

Day Four

Explore ❽ **Padstow** in the morning, and then cycle the Camel Trail to Wadebridge and back, ending with fish 'n' chips on ❾ **South Quay.**

Day Five

Walk across the fields to ❿ **Trevone,** and back to Padstow via the South West Coast Path, ending with a visit to ⓫ **Prideaux Place** (p 59, ❻).

Day Six

Drive west on the B3276 coast road via ⓬ **Bedruthan Steps** and ⓭ **Newquay** to ⓮ **St Agnes Head;** end the day at St Ives (44½ miles/71½km) (p 46).

Day Seven

Explore ⓯ **St Ives'** galleries in the morning; drive to ⓰ **Zennor** and the Wayside Museum (5 miles/8km) (p 54, ❿) and onto ⓱ **Cape Cornwall** to watch the sun set.

Helston from Coronation Park.

Day Eight

Drive to Penzance (8 miles/13km) and take the helicopter to the **18 Isles of Scilly** for the day (p 164); or spend the day exploring **19 Penzance** and **20 Marazion,** with a trip to St Michael's Mount (p 57, **1**).

Day Nine

Visit **21 Helston** (13½ miles/ 21¾km), then drive south on the A3083 to **22 Lizard Point** (11½ miles/18½km). Call in at the Seal Sanctuary at Gweek en route for Falmouth (p 37, **6**).

The Eden Project.

Day Ten

A day in **23 Falmouth:** visit the Maritime Museum in the morning, and then take the ferry to pictur-esque **24 St Mawes** and its castle (p 59, **4**).

Day Eleven

Explore the lovely gardens on the Helford river: **11 Carwinion** (p 29, **5**), **12 Glendurgan** (p 29, **6**) and **13 Trebah** (p 30, **7**) (4¼ miles/6¾km).

Day Twelve

Move on to **28 Lostwithiel** and Restormel Castle (37½ miles/60¼km); in the afternoon drive south to **29 Fowey** (7¼ miles/11½km) (p 105).

Day Thirteen

Follow the Forgotten Corner route (p 149) to **30 Polperro,** and then take the B3359/A390 back to Lost-withiel (7¼ miles).

Day Fourteen

Finish your 2-week tour with a visit to the **31 Eden Project** near St Austell (5¾ miles/9¼km). ●

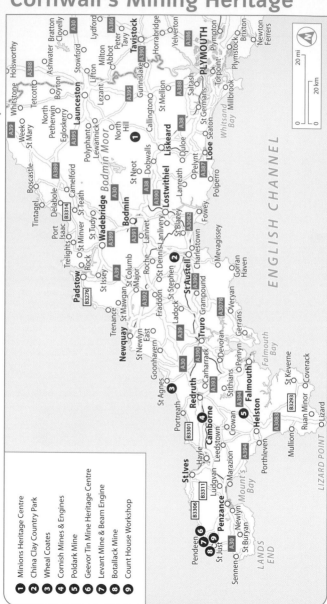

Cornwall's Mining Heritage

1 Minions Heritage Centre
2 China Clay Country Park
3 Wheal Coates
4 Cornish Mines & Engines
5 Poldark Mine
6 Geevor Tin Mine Heritage Centre
7 Levant Mine & Beam Engine
8 Botallack Mine
9 Count House Workshop

Previous page: Towanroath engine house.

'Wherever there's a hole in the ground you'll find a Cousin Jack at the bottom of it, searching for metal.' This 1881 quote from the son of a Wendron miner neatly sums up the significance of mining in Cornwall. The industry and its miners were once world renown, and the Cornish people are still justifiably proud of their tin- and copper-mining heritage, which reached its peak in the mid-19th century. The effects of the industry's demise on the economy and inhabitants of Cornwall were immense. In 2006, UNESCO established the Cornwall and West Devon Mining World Heritage Site in recognition of one of Europe's great industrial landscapes. **START: Minions Heritage Centre (5½ miles/8¾km) north of Liskeard). Trip Distance: 107 miles (171km). Trip Length: 2–3 days.**

Minions Heritage Centre.

❶ ★ Minions Heritage Centre.

A visit to Minions on Bodmin Moor gives you a blast of fresh air and an idea of how tough life once was in this part of Cornwall. This little village is the highest in Cornwall (300ft/ 984m above sea level). A former shanty town for itinerant miners, Minions is surrounded by the ruins of structures and buildings associated with the mining industry. The Heritage Centre occupies one of the engine houses of the South Phoenix mine. Tin-streaming –extracting ore from sifted streambed—material

began here in Roman times, and peaked in the 12th and 13th centuries. With the invention of the steam pumping engine in the early 18th century, deep mining for tin accelerated; at the peak of production 4000 men, women and children were employed in the Caradon Hill mines. Tin and copper mining ceased when the Prince of Wales shaft closed in 1914. The Cheesewring quarry just to the north of Minions provided granite for the Albert Memorial and Tower Bridge in London. 🕐 *45 min. Never busy. Minions PL14 5LL.* ☎ *01579 341463. Free admission. Open all year round.*

Turn right, signed to Liskeard. At Doublebois turn right on the A38 to Bodmin. At the roundabout before Bodmin keep ahead, then left on the A30 West for Redruth, and then the A391 St Austell. At the Carthew roundabout, keep ahead on the B3274 (brown signs). Distance: 24 miles (38½km).

❷ ★★ kids China Clay Country Park. No one travelling along the A30 can fail to notice the 'Cornish Alps', a jumble of strangely shaped, ghostly white peaks, which are spoil heaps from china clay quarries. China clay production is Cornwall's largest industry today, and the

Restored water wheel.

(1971) is still worked today. The Chinese had used kaolin (china clay, or decomposed granite) to make porcelain for centuries, but in 1768 William Cookworthy from Plymouth patented a method using local china clay. An excellent museum (audio-visual/interactive displays) leads to the Historic Trail, including a 35ft (10½m) water wheel (the largest working example in the county), settling tanks, chimneys and leats, and reconstructions of domestic life: clay worker's kitchen, cooperage and so on. The ½-mile (¾km) Nature Trail explores the grounds. 🕐 *4 hr. Wheal Martyn, Carthew, St Austell PL26 8XG.* ☎ *01726 850362. www. chinaclaycountrypark.co.uk. Adult £7.50, child (under 16) £4.50, family £20, concessions £6. Daily summer 10am–5pm, Nov–mid-Feb 10am–4pm, closed Jan–Feb Mon & Tues.*

China Clay Country Park (shop and café) lies within the old Gomm and Wheal Martin works (Wheal is Cornish for 'mine'). The Gomm works operated from about 1878 to the 1920s; Wheal Martyn dates from the 1820s, and the Wheal Martyn pit

Turn left on the B3274. At the roundabout turn left for Roche. Eventually bear right signed to the A30 Bodmin; join the A30 and head west to Redruth. Stay on

World Heritage Site, St Agnes.

the A30 until a roundabout (28 miles/45km) where St Agnes is signed (the B3277). At the edge of St Agnes, turn left signed The Beacon. Keep ahead at cross-roads, and then right on Beacon Drive. Park in Wheal Coates (National Trust (NT)) car park on the left. Distance: 33 miles (53km).

❸ ★ **Wheal Coates.** The north Cornish coastline around St Agnes is one of the most beautiful stretches of the South West Coast Path, made all the more impressive by the well-preserved and restored remains of Wheal Coates, dating from a phase of deep underground mining that began in the 1870s. The three large engine houses once contained Cornish beam engines; 138 people worked here in 1881. The Stamps and Whim engine house held the winding gear that hoisted ore from the 600ft- (183m) deep Towanroath shaft, and stamped (crushed) the ore for further processing; Towanroath engine house can be seen on the cliff edge below. The western gorse- and heather-covered heathland around the mine is scored with gullies and trenches, remnants of early opencast mining activity, and overlooked by St Agnes Beacon; legend has it that the Giant known as Bolster could stand with one foot on the Beacon and the other on Carn Brea above Redruth. This section of the coast, and the lovely beach at Porth Chapel just to the west of Wheal Coates, are now managed by the NT. ⏱ *45 min. St Agnes TR5 0NU. www.nationaltrust.org.uk. Free admission. Open all year round.*

Turn right; take the second lane right (at the phone box), signed to Porthtowan. At Towan Cross, turn right for Porthtowan, and then keep ahead signposted Portreath. Through Cambrose turn left on the B3300 to Redruth. At

the roundabout, turn right to Redruth/Camborne. Take the A3047 to Redruth West. At the next roundabout, keep ahead (brown tourist signs) on the A3047. Distance: 10 miles (16km).

❹ ★★★ **kids Cornish Mines & Engines.** You get a real understanding of the industrial and social history of Cornish mining here. The East Pool whim (winding) engine stands on Mitchell's shaft (1500ft/457m deep); East Pool is Cornwall's oldest mine (and was closed in 1947). Climb the steps and watch the last steam-powered rotative beam engine made in Cornwall in action. Across the road (through a supermarket's car park) you'll find the Industrial Discovery Centre in Taylor's Shaft compressor house (1922), which supplied compressed air to nearby underground workings; it has a remarkable collection of mining memorabilia and wonderful working models of Cornish mines. A fascinating film covers the industry's history, and displays/

Stamps engine house.

recordings tell the miner's story: the 1841 household accounts of one miner record that he earned 14 shillings [70£] a week, his three children brought in 4s 6d [22.5£], and that after essential outlays the family had just 2 shillings [20£] left for food and clothing. Children as young as 6-years-old were sent to work in the mines. 🕑 *2 hr. Pool, Redruth TR15 3NP. ☎ 01209 315027. www.national trust.org.uk. Adult £6.40, child £3.20, family (2 adults) £16, family (1 adult) £9.60. 19 Mar–30 Jun & 1 Sept–1 Nov Mon, Wed, Thurs, Sun 11am–5pm; 1 July–31 Aug Mon, Wed, Thurs, Fri, Sat, Sun 11am–5pm. NT members free.*

Turn right on the B3047, and follow the signs for Falmouth/Helston. Turn right on the A393 and then right on the B3300 Helston. Turn left on the B3297 Helston. In Trenear, turn left as signed. Distance: 13 miles (21km).

⑤ ★ kids Poldark Mine. If you're a mining heritage devotee you may

Cliff-top chimney.

Working model of a tin mine.

be surprised by the myriad of attractions designed to occupy children near the entrance to the Poldark Mine; but don't be put off, the hour-long tour of the mine is completely fascinating, giving a real insight into what working conditions must have been like for Cornwall's miners. It's not for the nervous or claustrophobic (or children under 5), and involves a scramble along narrow rough-hewn tunnels and walkways, accompanied by sounds of running water (and occasional drips) to a final depth of almost 150ft (46m). The mine was worked from 1710 to 1790. An excellent museum details the history of tin mining, and also contains the last working Cornish beam engine in the county (formerly used to pump water from the mine, it was decommissioned in 1959). 🕑 *2 hr; very busy in school holidays. Trenear, Wendron, Helston TR13 0ES. ☎ 01326 573173. www. poldark-mine.co.uk. Adult £8, child (ages 5–16) £5, family £20, concessions £7.60. Daily mid-July–end Aug*

10am–5:30pm; Sept–end Nov & mid-Apr–mid-July, closed Sat.

Turn left on the B3297 to Helston. Follow signs for Lizard, and then turn right onto the A394 Penzance. On meeting the A30 (15 miles/24km), follow signs for Penzance and then pick up the A30 to Lands End. Turn right on the A3071 St Just, and then right on the B3318 Pendeen (brown tourist sign). Turn left on the B3306 to Trewellard. Distance: 25 miles (40km).

⑥ ★★ kids Geevor Tin Mine Heritage Centre. One of Cornwall's last working tin mines, Geevor finally closed in 1990, but has cleverly re-invented itself as a fascinating 'attraction'. It's the largest mining heritage site in the UK, with over 2 acres (¾ hectare) of mine buildings and a new world-class museum, opened in October 2008. Geevor has something of the *Marie Celeste* about it, as if the 400 miners have just laid down their tools and gone home; it feels like a real working mine, and used to extend to a depth of 3,000ft (914m). Don't miss the underground tour, usually led by an ex-employee, or the excellent 'Time Trek', which traces the history of Cornwall and the tin-mining industry since prehistoric times. Take a walk through the workings to look at the coast, where the cliffs are stained green by copper deposits. Note that the café and shop can be accessed without going into the main site, and that the South West Coast Path can be reached even when the site is closed (if

you arrive when the site is open make sure that you park above the metal gate to avoid getting locked into the car park). ⏰ *3 hr; big site so rarely crowded. Pendeen TR19 7EW.* ☎ *01736 788662. www.geevor.com. Adult £8.50, child over 5 £4.50, family £25, concessions £7.50. Daily 10am–4pm (except Sat).*

You can take a short walk along the coast to reach the Levant Mine: follow signs past the Geevor café and shop, and then bear left to reach the coast path and Levant. Or you can drive south on the B3306 for a short distance and then follow the signs right to find the car park on the cliff-top. Distance: ½ mile (¾km).

⑦ ★★ Levant Mine & Beam Engine. Levant Mine started as a copper mine around 1820, and from the mid-19th century produced tin; at one time the workings extended for 1 mile (1½km) out under the sea. It was the site of a horrific disaster in 1919, when a lifting device collapsed and killed 31 miners. The mine closed in 1930, and today is owned by the NT and operated by the Trevithick Society. Time your visit for one of the 'steaming' days, when the restored beam engine (the oldest in Cornwall) can be seen working. ⏰ *1 hr; rarely crowded. Trewellard, Pendeen TR19 7SX.* ☎ *01736 786156. www.nationaltrust. org.uk. Adult £5.80, child (ages 5–16) £2.90, family £14.50, family (1 adult) £8.70. NT members free. Open (steaming)*

Geevor can be accessed from the South West Coast Path.

Remains of Levant Mine count house.

daily Mar 11am–5pm; early Apr–end May–end Oct Wed and Fri; Jun Wed, Thurs, Fri, Sun; July–Sept Tue, Wed, Thurs, Fri.

Levant mine.

Turn right onto the B3306. At Botallack, turn right on the corner and right at the next junction. Follow the unmade lane past Botallack Count House to parking area; walk towards the coast. Distance: 2 miles (3¼km).

8 ★ Botallack Mine. No tour of Cornwall's mining heritage sites would be complete without a trip to the coast at Botallack, if only for the coastal views. The cliffs are scattered with all kinds of derelict buildings, chimneys and so on, but the most romantic mine remains are the famous cliff-clinging Crowns engine houses, featured on many a postcard and calendar. The Crowns mine was pretty well worked out by the late 19th century, but reopened for arsenic production from 1907 to 1914. **9 Count House Workshop** (NT) contains historical displays and can also be visited. ⏱ *30 min. Botallack.* ☎ *01736 788588. Free admission. Open all year round 10am–4pm.*

The Crowns, Botallack Mine.

Self-catering Options

If you're planning a lengthy stay in Cornwall, consider self-catering. Many hotels and B&Bs refuse 1-night bookings in high season, although many offer reduced rates for 3 nights or more and good-value dinner-and-B&B packages. Note that in the high season prices rise sharply and self-catering accommodation has to be booked for a minimum 1-week stay.

Self-catering prices vary considerably, depending on whether you're renting a fixed mobile home (from £200 per week) or a luxury cottage with swimming pool (£450–1,800 per week). In general, however, the standard of rentable holiday accommodation in Cornwall is extremely high. If you know which area you want to visit, type the name of the nearest town/village into your Internet search engine and follow links to 'accommodation': if you want to stay on a working farm, try www.cornishfarmholidays.co.uk or www.farmstay.co.uk; also try www.helpfulholidays.com, www.holidaycottages.co.uk, www.toadhallcottages.co.uk, www.cornwall-online.co.uk, www.nationaltrustcottages.co.uk, www.landmarktrust.org.uk and the official website of the Cornwall Tourist Board, www.visitcornwall.com. Trinity House lighthouse cottages at St Anthony Head, Pendeen and Trevose Head can be booked via www.ruralretreats.co.uk. The regional websites in The Savvy Traveller are also an excellent source of information.

Cornwall's Gardens

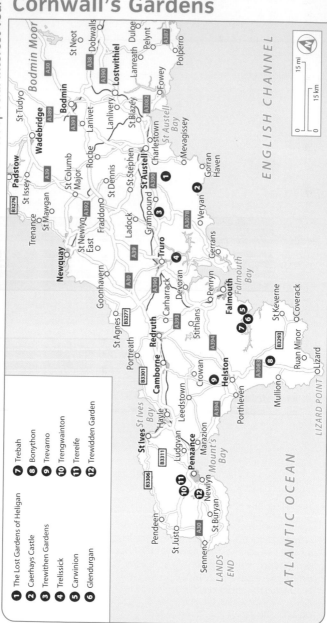

1. The Lost Gardens of Heligan
2. Caerhays Castle
3. Trewithen Gardens
4. Trelissick
5. Carwinion
6. Glendurgan
7. Trebah
8. Bonython
9. Trevarno
10. Trengwainton
11. Tereife
12. Trewidden Garden

Splendid gardens can be found all over Cornwall, some privately owned with specialist plant collections and limited opening times, others in the care of the National Trust. But the greatest concentration are found in the wonderfully equable climate of Cornwall's sheltered south coast, warmed by the Gulf Stream. Here spring arrives early, and frosts or snow are rare. Flowers bloom all year, including many tender subtropical species unable to thrive outdoors in other parts of the UK. For more information on Cornish gardens get hold of the free Cornwall Gardens Guide (from Tourist Information Centres) or visit the following websites: www.gardensof cornwall.com and www.greatgardensofcornwall.co.uk. **START: Helligan (Pentewan, 3¾ miles/6km south of St Austell). Trip distance: 80 miles (128km). Trip length: 6–7 days.**

❶ ★★★ KIDS The Lost Gardens of Heligan. Heligan, seat of the Tremayne family for 400 years, hit the headlines in 1990 when the 'lost gardens' were rediscovered and restored by Tim Smit (better known as the creator of the Eden Project). The gardens, originally laid out between 1770 and 1914, fell into neglect after World War I, when most of the staff were killed. It's a big site consisting of around 200 acres (81 hectares) of gardens, woodland and meadow. Allow plenty of time (or several visits) to see it: it's a long and strenuous walk to the farthest extremities (such as the Lost Valley and the subtropical Jungle), but more formal areas lie within easy reach of the café and visitor centre. These include: the Victorian Pleasure Grounds, with a grotto and wishing well; the Ravine, a giant rockery; and the walled Victorian vegetable garden, where over 200 varieties of 'heritage' fruit, vegetables, salads and herbs are produced. Don't miss the melon yard and pineapple pit, and Lobbs' excellent farm shop on site. ⏱ *5 hr. Pentewan, St Austell PL26 6EN. ☎ 01726 845100. www. heligan.com. Adult £8.50, child (ages 6–16) £5, family £23.50, concessions £7.50. Daily Apr–Sept 10am–6pm, Oct–Mar 10am–5pm.*

In the depths at Heligan.

Turn left, signed Gorran Haven; turn right at Gorran High Lanes (3 miles/4¾km) signed to Caerhays. Turn right as signposted. Distance: 4½ miles (7¼km).

❷ ★★ Caerhays Castle. The present Gothic-looking building (you may recognise it as the stand-in for Manderley in Hitchcock's film version of *Rebecca*) overlooking Porthluney Cove was constructed in the mid-19th century, but the estate

Caerhays Castle and gardens.

dates back to the 14th century, when it was owned by the Trevanion family. J.C. Williams inherited the estate from his father in 1880 and was responsible for many improvements to the layout of the grounds, including the informal woodland gardens, at their best in spring when camellias, magnolias (it holds the National Magnolia Collection) and rhododendrons are in bloom. ⏱ *2 hr. Gorran, St Austell PL26 6LY.* ☎ *01872 501310. www.caerhays. co.uk. Adult £5.50, child (ages 6–16) £2.50, concessions £5. Daily mid-Feb–end May 10am–5pm.*

Turn right from the castle; pick up the signs for Grampound. Turn right on the B3287; after ½ mile (¾km), keep straight on. Turn left on the A390 through Grampound; turn left as signed. Distance: 8¾ miles (14km).

❸ ★★ **Trewithen Gardens.** This historic private estate is one of the loveliest in Cornwall, famous for its collection of camellias, magnolias, rhododendrons and rare species—and its lovely woodland walks. The 18th-century house is considered to be one of the finest of its period in the county. More than 1,500 varieties of plants, trees and shrubs are on sale at the nursery. ⏱ *4 hr. Grampound Road, Truro TR2 4DD.* ☎ *01726 883647. www.trewithen gardens.co.uk. Adult £5, child (ages 6–16) £2.50 Mar–Jun, free July–Aug. Early Mar–end Sept Mon–Sat 10am–4:30pm, Mar–May Sun.*

Turn left on the A390 signed Truro (7 miles/11¼km). Pick up the signs for the A39 Falmouth; at second roundabout at Playing Place (4 miles/6½km), turn left (brown sign), and then turn left onto the B3269. Distance: 13 miles (21km).

❹ ★★ **kids** **Trelissick.** One of the best things about Trelissick is its glorious setting on the Carrick Roads, with a large expanse of open parkland and a network of scenic footpaths along the wooded banks of the River Fal. You'll find lots of locals here exercising their dogs (and children). Trelissick also has 20 acres (8 hectares) of formal gardens featuring rhododendrons, camellias, azaleas, magnolias and tree ferns. The King Harry Ferry serves the gardens from Truro, Falmouth and St Mawes (May–Sept; (p 63). ⏱ *2 hr; also extensive walks through estate. Feock, nr Truro TR3 6QL. ☎ 01872 862090. www.nationaltrust.org.uk. Adult £7, child (ages 6–16) £3.50, family £17.50; NT members free. Daily early–mid-Feb, Nov–Dec 11am– 4pm, mid-Feb–end Oct 10:30am– 5:30pm.*

Return to the B3289; turn right and then left onto the A39 (Falmouth). At the Hillhead roundabout (10 miles/16km) turn right (brown signs), and then left (Mawnan Smith). At crossroads turn left; in Mawnan Smith bear left (brown sign). Distance: 14¼ miles (23km).

❺ ★ Carwinion. Exploring the gardens at Carwinion is a refreshingly informal experience. It's as if you've dropped in to visit friends or take a cream tea on the terrace. The house is a modest but charming 18th-century manor, whose gardens

drop to the Helford river. Carwinion has belonged to the Rogers family for many years; they and their cousins, the Foxes of Glendurgan (see ❻ below), were Victorian plant hunters. Today both gardens show the benefits of that legacy. The present owners have spent 30 years restoring the delightfully unmanicured 12-acre (4¾-hectare) garden— a jungly collection of bamboos, camellias, hydrangeas, ferns and exotics. ⏱ *2 hr. Mawnan Smith, Falmouth TR11 5JA. ☎ 01326 250258. www.carwiniion.co.uk. Adult £4, child (under 16) free, concessions £4. Daily all year 10am–5:30pm.*

Turn left into Mawnan Smith, and then left (brown sign). Distance: ¾ mile (1¼km).

❻ ★★ kids Glendurgan. A lovely subtropical valley garden with many exotic species that runs steeply down to the Helford river and Durgan hamlet (take the return climb slowly!). The garden was created by Alfred Fox, a prosperous shipping merchant, in the 1820s. It contains magnificent displays of magnolias

Carwinion House.

Tresco Abbey Gardens

If you have the stamina for even more subtropical gardens, take a daytrip to the island of Tresco in the Isles of Scilly (p 164) to visit the Abbey Gardens, created in the 19th century by Augustus Smith, who took over the lease of the islands from the Duchy of Cornwall in 1834. This is a truly magical place, where you can wander through a maze of narrow paths and terraces, admiring exotic species gathered by Smith from all over the world including the Mediterranean, South Africa, California, New Zealand and the Canaries. The gardens are charmingly eccentric too, full of murals, grottos and statues. The Valhalla Museum contains a collection of ships' figureheads and memorabilia from numerous shipwrecks. **British International** operates helicopter flights (around £100) from Penzance direct to Tresco all year round (weather permitting) (☎ 01736 363871; www.islesofscillyhelicopter.com). ⏱ 3 hr. Tresco Abbey Gardens, Tresco TR24 0QQ. ☎ 01720 424108. www.tresco.co.uk. Daily 10am–4pm. Adult £10, child (under 16) free, weekly ticket £20.

and camellias in spring, impressive trees, exotic plants and carpets of wild flowers. Children will enjoy getting lost in the huge laurel maze (planted in 1833) and trying out the

Rhododendron in full bloom.

Giant's Stride rope swing, as well as the little sandy beach at Durgan. A ferry service links Glendurgan with Helford village and Trebah (see ❼ below). ⏱ *3 hr. Mawnan Smith, Falmouth TR11 5JZ.* ☎ *01326 250906. www.nationaltrust,org.uk. Adult £6.40, child (ages 6–16) £3.20, family £16; NT members free. Mid-Feb–end July, Sept–Oct Tues–Sat 10:30am–5:30pm, Aug daily (except Sun).*

Turn left to find Trebah on the left. Distance: ¼ mile (½km).

❼ ★★★ **kids** **Trebah.** 'Trebah' is a Celtic name meaning 'the house on the bay'. This 26-acre (10½-hectare) subtropical paradise in a wooded ravine has a great sense of history. It was first planted over 160 years ago, and opened to the public in 1987. Many consider it to be one of the leading gardens of the world. Streams and waterfalls cascade down the valley to the Helford river; there are huge tree ferns, bamboos, giant gunnera and rhododendrons.

A terrific programme of activities for children is put on during holiday periods. ⏱ *3 hr. Mawnan Smith, Falmouth TR 11 5JKZ.* ☎ *01326 252200. www.trebah-garden.co.uk. Adult £7.50, child (ages 5–15) £2.50, concessions £6.50. Nov–end Feb half-price admission, off-season deal to NT/RHS members. Daily 10:30am–5pm (or dusk).*

Turn left; pick up the signs for Constantine (narrow road); turn left through the village. Turn left, signed Gweek, and left again. Through Gweek, pick up the signs for Helston; at junction turn right, and then left for the A3083 signed Lizard. At Cury Cross Lanes, turn left as signed; garden is on right. Distance: 11¼ miles (18km).

❽ ★ Bonython. Bonython's 20 acres (8 hectares) of lovely gardens, parkland and lakes surround a Georgian manor tucked away on the Lizard Peninsula. The gardens lay dormant for 150 years until they were restored in the late 1990s; today they are famous for their

King Protea.

View of Trebah from the lower lake.

year-round colour. Other attractions include an 18th-century walled garden with herbaceous borders, a potager garden of flowers and vegetables, and an orchard containing Cornish varieties of apple trees. ⏱ *2 hr. Cury Cross Lanes, Helston TR12 7BA.* ☎ *01326 240550. www. bonythonmanor.co.uk. Adult £6, child (ages 6–16) £2, family £14. Apr–Sept Mon–Fri 10am–4:30pm.*

Retrace your route to the A3083; turn right to Helston and at roundabout turn left onto the A394 (Penzance). After 2 miles (3¼km), turn right (brown sign) onto the B3302. Turn right onto the B3303, right as signed and right into garden. Distance: 8¾ miles (14km).

❾ ★★★ kids Trevarno. You get a lot for your money at Trevarno: 70 acres (28 hectares) of wonderful gardens and grounds to explore (lake, Victorian boathouse, sunken Italian garden, yew tunnel, formal and woodland areas, rockery, grotto and more), a lovely 1¼ mile (2km) estate walk with views towards the coast, the National Museum of Gardening (a fascinating collection of gardening memorabilia), Vintage Toy Museum, and a Soap Museum with organic skincare products on sale. After all this, you may need to relax with some refreshment in the Fountain Garden conservatory. To top it all Trevarno is also a World Heritage Site Visitor Attraction with historic connections to the Cornish mining industry. During 2009 a section of the disused Helston railway branch line running through the estate was restored (trips are planned). ⏲ *5 hr. Crowntown, Helston TR13 0RU.* ☎ *01326 574274. www. trevarno.co.uk. Adult £6.50, child (ages 5–14) £2.25, family £16, concessions £3.25–5.75. Daily 10:30am–5pm.*

Retrace your route to the A394; turn right (Penzance). After 9 miles (14½km) join the A30 (Penzance). Follow the A30 round the edge of Penzance; at the Heamoor roundabout, turn right (brown sign) and then left as signed. Distance: 16 miles (25½km).

❿ ★★ kids **Trengwainton.** These gardens prove beyond doubt that this part of Cornwall enjoys the mildest climate in the UK. Sir Rose Price, a sugar planter with interests in Jamaica, first laid out the gardens in the early 19th century, creating a series of small walled compartments with unique raised beds, ideal for growing tender plants. When Lt Col Edward Bolitho inherited the gardens in 1925, he started to fill these miniature 'garden rooms' with exotic species gathered on overseas plant-hunting expeditions. Today the gardens display a magnificent collection of plants and shrubs gathered from all over the world: including Burma, China, Chile, New Zealand and Australia. You can see the walled gardens best from a raised platform. Trengwainton also has fine collections of bamboos, grasses and tree ferns, and bog plants growing beside the picturesque stream running the entire length of the gardens. There are splendid views of Mount's Bay

Old potting shed, Trevarno.

Peacocks abound at Trevarno!

from the terrace. 🕐 *3 hr. Madron, nr Penzance TR20 8RZ.* 📞 *01736 363148. www.nationaltrust.org.uk. Adult £5.80, child (ages 6–16) £2.90, family £14.50, NT members free. Daily (except Fri and Sat) early Feb– end Oct 10:30am–5pm.*

Retrace your route to the A30; turn right (Lands End). Distance: 2 miles (3¼km).

⓫ ★★ kids Trereife. Trereife is one of Cornwall's finest Queen Anne houses, dating from the early 18th century. The present owner is a descendant of Charles Valentine le Grice, who moved into Trengwainton in 1798.The gardens are steadily being restored—in 1999 an elaborate parterre was planted with azaleas, rhododendrons and camellias, many of which were first established in the 1920s–30s. 🕐 *3 hr. Newlyn, Penzance TR20 8TS.* 📞 *01736 362750. www. trereifepark.co.uk. Adult £5.75, child (ages 5–14) £2.50, family £14, conces- sions £4.25; gardens only £3. Daily (except Sun) 11am–5pm.*

Turn right onto the A30 towards Lands End. Distance: ½ mile (¾km).

⓬ ★★ kids Trewidden Garden. Originally planted by T.B. Bolitho in the late 19th century, Trewidden's manageable 15-acre (6-hectare) gardens boast a fabulous array of magnolias and camellias. The impressive Tree Fern Dell, holds one of the largest collections of the Australian tree fern in the northern hemisphere. The walled garden has been recently renovated and the south gardens extended; there are delightful water features and a maze of paths to explore. 🕐 *3 hr. Buryas Bridge, Penzance TR20 8TT.* 🕐 *01736 351979. www.trewiddengarden. co.uk. Adult £5, child (under 16) free. Daily July–Aug, early Feb–end Sept Wed–Sun 10:30am–5:30pm.*

Cornwall for all the Family

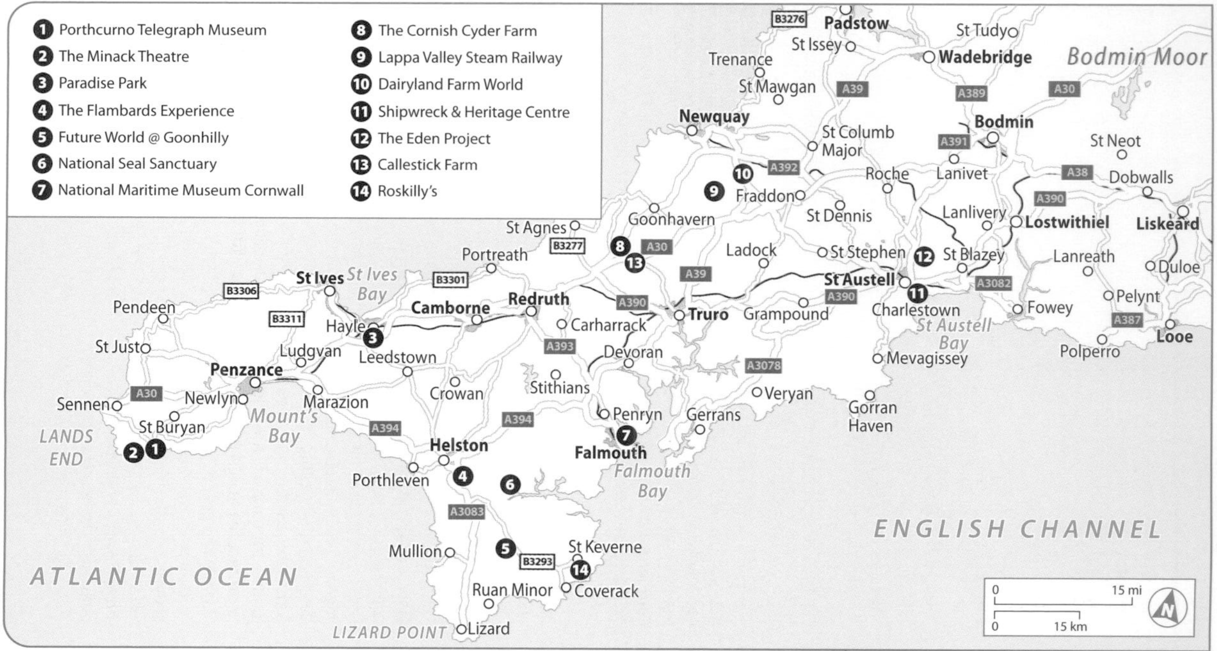

1 Porthcurno Telegraph Museum
2 The Minack Theatre
3 Paradise Park
4 The Flambards Experience
5 Future World @ Goonhilly
6 National Seal Sanctuary
7 National Maritime Museum Cornwall
8 The Cornish Cyder Farm
9 Lappa Valley Steam Railway
10 Dairyland Farm World
11 Shipwreck & Heritage Centre
12 The Eden Project
13 Callestick Farm
14 Roskilly's

ENGLISH CHANNEL

ATLANTIC OCEAN

0   15 mi
0   15 km

F ew would disagree that Cornwall is one of Britain's very best family holiday destinations, as the massive southwesterly human migration in high summer clearly indicates. Thousands of families head here every year, many parents reliving the magic of their own childhood memories spent paddling in rock pools and feeling soft Cornish sand between their toes. Somehow, on those holidays, the sun was always shining. Fine weather can't be guaranteed in Cornwall, even in summer, but that maritime Gulf Stream climate is undeniably balmy. Teamed with a stack of first-rate attractions and adventure sports, plus a fine choice of places to eat and stay, it isn't hard to see why Cornwall's appeal persists from one generation to the next. The high-profile Eden Project, opened in March 2001, re-established Cornwall as a 'must visit' destination for old and young alike. **START: Porthcurno Telegraph Museum (Porthcurno, 3 miles/4¾km east of Lands End). Trip distance: 97 miles (156km). Trip length: 5 days.**

❶ ★★ Porthcurno Telegraph Museum. The coastline west of Lamorna is especially picturesque, a series of sandy coves tucked beneath jagged cliffs. The scattered hamlet of Porthcurno offers more than pretty scenery, however. For nearly a century, it was one of the UK's leading telecommunications centres, at the hub of the Eastern Telegraph Company's international network. From 1870 onwards, undersea cables ran into the bay from all over the world. In World War II it played a vital role as a secret communications centre. Today the Telegraph Museum— 'home of the Victorian Internet'—is open to the public. Here, among vintage speaking tubes of mahogany and brass, you can learn about the history of telegraphic communication and visit the underground tunnels constructed in World War II to protect the telegraph station from bombing raids. ⏱ *3 hr. Porthcurno TR19 6JX.* ☎ *01736 810966. www.porthcurno.org.uk. Adult £5.50, child (ages 5–16) £3.10, family £13.20, concessions £4.90. Daily early Apr–early Nov 10am– 5pm, early Nov–late Mar Sun & Mon.*

Minack Theatre, southwest Cornwall.

❷ Minack Theatre sits on the granite cliffs 200ft (61m) above Porthcurno beach. This extraordinary venture was the brain-child of the single-minded Rowena Cade, who with the help of two gardeners in 1932 carved a classically styled amphitheatre from the bare rock. A performance at this spectacular open-air venue during its summer season is unforgettable (book ahead for tickets; the show goes on come rain or shine—savvy theatre-goers bring rugs and cushions). The theatre site and café are open to the public

Rainbow parakeets, Paradise Park.

outside performance times. ⏱ *1½ hr. Porthcurno TR19 6JU.* ☎ *01736 810181. www.minack.com. Adult £3.50, child [12–16] £1.40, over-60s £2.50. Daily Apr–May 9:30am–5pm, Jun–late Sept Mon, Tues, Thurs, Sat & Sun 9:30am–5:30pm, Wed, Fri 9:30–11:30am. Call for winter opening.*

Turn right from car park onto the B3315. Turn right (to Penzance). Meet the A30 after 6 miles (9¾km); turn right (to Penzance). Follow the A30 round Penzance, picking up signs for the A30 Redruth/Hayle. After 15 miles (24km) take the second exit off the roundabout (brown signs) Hayle B3301. In Hayle, turn right onto the B3302 (Helston); follow the signs to Paradise Park. Distance: 17 miles (27½km).

❸ ★★★ **Paradise Park.** This wildlife conservation centre was established in 1973 as a tropical bird garden, but has expanded considerably since, adding attractions such as a huge indoor play barn and Jungle Express train. It occupies the walled garden of a Victorian house in the centre of Hayle, and the enclosures are surrounded by luxuriant subtropical vegetation. Children will love the brightly coloured rainbow parakeets (you can enter their enclosure and help to feed them) as well as penguins and otters, pandas and native red squirrels. One of the centre's star attractions is the rare red-legged Cornish chough, a crow-like bird which returned to breed on south Cornwall's cliffs in 2001 after an absence of many years; the first chicks for 50 years hatched in 2002. ⏱ *4 hr; very busy in peak holiday times. 16 Trelissick Road, Hayle TR27 4HB.* ☎ *01736 751020. www.paradisepark.org.uk. Adult £10.99, child (ages 3–15) £8.99, family £38.50, concessions £7.99. Daily summer 10am–5pm, spring/autumn 10am–4pm, winter 10am–3pm.*

Return to the B3302 and turn right (Helston). After 8½ miles (13¾km) turn left onto the A394 (Helston). Follow the A394 round the edge of Helston; at roundabout, turn left for Falmouth (A394) (brown signs) and then turn right after 180 yards (200m). Distance: 10 miles (16km).

❹ ★★★ **The Flambards Experience.** This is a great place for all-round (and just as importantly, all-weather!) family entertainment. Older children will go for the 'thrill' rides, such as the Hornet Rollercoaster and Canyon River Log Flume, while youngsters may prefer the gentler Cornish Mine Train and Tea Cup Ride. You can have close encounters with spiders, snakes, owls and lizards, and have fun with gravity, light and sound. Grandparents can stroll down a Victorian shopping street, wander through a re-creation of Britain in the Blitz or trace the history of aviation. The complex is set in beautiful landscaped gardens. ⏱ *4 hr; busy in peak holiday times. Clodgey Lane,*

Helston TR13 0QA. ☎ *01326 573404.* *www.flambards.co.uk. Adult £16.50, child (under 16) and seniors £11.50. Daily 10am–5pm (later in high summer). Call for winter opening.*

Return to the A394; turn left, soon following the A3083 for Lizard (brown tourist sign). Just beyond the RNAS Culdrose air-sea rescue base, turn left as signed on the B3293 (St Keverne). Follow the brown tourist signs. Distance: 6 miles (9¾km).

❺ ★★ Future World @ Goonhilly. Goonhilly rises out of the heathlands of the Lizard Peninsula like some sci-fi movie set. At one time, it was the world's largest satellite station, with over 60 dishes pointing into space; the site now houses an excellent multimedia visitor centre. In its operational heyday Goonhilly sent and received millions of telephone calls, TV pictures, faxes and Internet connections, and was the first 'earth station' to receive live TV images from America. Today the Future World experience offers a look back at 200 years of communications' history, and an idea of what might happen in the future. A guided tour of the site, visiting Arthur (the most venerable of the satellite dishes), is highly recommended. Plenty of hands-on activities to keep children occupied, plus there's a children's play area, nature tours and film show. ⏱ *3 hr. Helston TR12 6LQ.* ☎ *0800 679593. www.goonhilly.bt.com. Adult £7.95, child (ages 5–16) £5.95, family (2 adults) £26, family (1 adult) £19, concessions £7.25. Extra charge for site tour. Spring/autumn 10am–5pm, summer 6pm. Call for winter opening.*

Turn left on the B3293. After 2 miles (3¼km) at the roundabout in Garras keep ahead, signed Gweek. Turn right at the next junction; cross the bridge and turn right as signposted. Follow signs. Distance: 4½ miles (7¼km).

❻ ★★ National Seal Sanctuary. Seals are difficult creatures to spot in their natural habitat, but here you can get up close and personal with these irresistible animals. The centre rescues and rehabilitates sick and injured seals from all over the country. There are pups and seals on view, as well as lots of information on seals worldwide. The seal pools are about a 10-minute walk from the entrance, but a Safari bus shuttles back and forth in season. Feeding times are especially popular, and there's more to watch

Laidback seal at Gweek Seal Sanctuary.

The National Maritime Museum.

in the sea-lion lagoon and otter creek, too. ⏱ *3 hr. Gweek, nr Helston TR12 6UG.* ☎ *01326 221361. www.sealsanctuary.co.uk. Adult £13, child (ages 3–14) £10, concessions £11. Daily 9am–5pm.*

Return to the bridge and turn right towards Falmouth. After 7½ miles (12km), turn right (Penryn/Truro). At the next roundabout turn right and then almost immediately left

Innovative displays in the National Maritime Museum.

(to Falmouth). At traffic lights turn right onto the A39 (town centre). Bear left down Avenue Road (brown tourist signs) for town centre and Maritime Museum parking. Distance: 10 miles (16km).

7 ★★★ National Maritime Museum Cornwall. Whether or not you're interested in boats, there's something for everyone at this museum—give yourself enough time to take it all in. By any standards it's a highly impressive attraction, from the innovative design of the waterfront building to the imaginative display of the exhibits: many of the boats are suspended on wires in a huge central atrium, surrounded by multi-level walkways. The Lookout tower offers amazing views over Falmouth Bay and the docks, and you can have fun sailing a remote-controlled dinghy on an indoor lake, with frustrating shifting 'winds'. There are hands-on displays to entertain the whole family, and a phenomenal amount of information on boats, weather patterns, sail making and boat building. Children (of all ages) will love it. ⏱ *4 hr; popular attraction but spacious. Discovery Quay, Falmouth TR11 3QY.* ☎ *01326 313388. www.nmmc.co.uk.*

Adult £8.75, child (ages 6–15) £6, family £24, concessions £6. Daily 10am–5pm.

Follow the 'outbound traffic' signs, soon picking up signs to the A39 Truro. After 11 miles (17¾km), at Arch Hill roundabout (Truro), turn left onto the A390 (Redruth). Reach the A30 at Chivenor's Cross; take the A3075 (to Newquay). After 9½ miles (15km), turn right as signed. Distance: 20 miles (32km).

❽ ★★ The Cornish Cyder Farm.

This is a fun place, with ciders, perries and fruit juices on sale. Around 150 years ago, the custom was for farm workers to be paid in cider at the rate of 4–5 pints (approximately 2¼–2¾ litres) a day, and the farm's slogan 'Legless but happy' sums up the relaxed atmosphere. A guided tour explains the cider-making process, and bumpy tractor-and-trailer rides take visitors through the orchards. It's a working farm, with animals on view. ⏱ *3 hr. Penhallow, Truro TR4 9LW. ☎ 01872 573356. www.thecornishcyderfarm. co.uk. Admission free; guided tours adult £6.50, child (6–16) £4.50, family £16, concessions £5.50. Daily Apr–Dec 9/10am to 4–8pm, depending on season.*

Return to the A3075; turn right (to Newquay). After 5 miles (8km), turn right as signed (to St Newlyn East). In village, bear left as signed (brown signs). Distance: 8 miles (13km).

❾ ★★★ Lappa Valley Steam Railway.

I really enjoyed this 'Magical Mystery Tour'. The experience begins with a delightful 1-mile (1½km) steam-train ride along the narrow-gauge Lappa Valley line to East Wheal Rose, a former tin-mining site transformed into a family attraction. Go canoeing on the lake, take a ride on two miniature railways, picnic in the family games field and try out the pedal cars. There's a restored engine house and lots of information on the history of the site; trains run every 40 minutes in the peak season. ⏱ *5 hr; busy at peak holiday times but large site. St Newlyn East, nr Newquay TR8 5LX. ☎ 01872 510317. www.lappavalley. co.uk. Adult £9.50, child (ages 3–15) £7.50, family £30, concessions £7.80; off-peak prices reduced. Daily Apr–end Oct; first train 10:30am; Oct closed Mon, Fri, Sat.*

Turn right; at the T-junction, turn right to meet the A3058; turn left and travel about 360 yards (400m). Distance: 2 miles (3¼km).

❿ ★★ Dairyland Farm World.

This large site has many different attractions: several play areas, animal petting, tractor rides, nature trails and an assault course. It is still a working farm, where you can watch dairy cows being milked in an extraordinary space-age orbiter (the first of its kind in Europe) and learn

Lappa Valley steam train.

Traditional tall ship, Charlestown.

more about milk production. There are excellent displays of Victorian agricultural and household equipment, plus a Cornish heritage centre. ⏱ *4 hr. Nr Newquay TR8 5AA.* ☎ *01872 510246. www.dairyland farmworld.co.uk. Adult/child over 3ft (91cm) £7.95, family £33, concessions £6.20. Daily Apr–end Oct 10am–5pm; reduced opening in winter (call for details).*

Turn left onto the A3058 (to St Austell). After nearly 11 miles (17¾km), meet the A390 in St Austell; turn left (to Liskeard). Pick up brown signs at the large roundabout; turn right onto the A3061 (to Charlestown). Distance: 13 miles (21km).

⓫ ★★ **Shipwreck & Heritage Centre.** Walk around the old port of Charlestown and you'll step into history. The lovely Georgian terraces and cobbled quayside are unchanged since the 18th century, and tall ships sit in the harbour. Charlestown contains the largest private collection of shipwreck and maritime memorabilia in Europe. The visitor centre has an old-fashioned feel, stuffed with all manner of fascinating bits and pieces, and finding your way around the maze of small rooms is an adventure in itself. ⏱ *2 hr (but allow time for looking round Charlestown as well). Quay Road, Charlestown, nr St Austell PL25 3NJ.* ☎ *01726 69897. www.shipwreck charlestown.com. Adult £5.80, child (over 10) £2.90, concessions £3.85. Daily Mar–end Oct 10am–5pm.*

Return to the A390 and turn right (to Liskeard), After 1 mile (1½km) turn left onto the A391 (Bodmin) (brown tourist signs). At the roundabout in Carluddon, turn right and follow signs. Distance: 6 miles (9¾km).

⓬ ★★★ **The Eden Project.** The Eden Project is in a state of constant evolution and has been ever since it first opened in March 2001; there's something new to see on every visit. Constructed in a 160-year-old china clay quarry, the Eden Project is famed for its huge iconic 'biomes' (geodesic domes that reproduce conditions found in the humid

Traditional tall ship prow.

Mediterranean Biome and The Core at Eden.

tropics and warm temperate zones): here you can walk through the equivalent of an Amazon rainforest. The project's message combines conservation and education, exploring human's dependence on natural resources. Visitors come away with a better understanding of how vital a healthy natural world is to our survival—and the information is absorbed in an engaging way. 🕐 *5 hr; go early to avoid long entry queues; huge site. Bodelva, Cornwall PL24 2SG. ☎ 01726 811911. www.eden project.com. Adult £16, child (under 16) £5, family £38, concessions £8. Daily 9am–6pm.*

Cornish Ice Cream

Turn right from the Cornish Cyder Farm and within minutes you reach ⓫ **Callestick Farm,** where you can find some of Cornwall's most delicious homemade ice cream: 'pure Cornish indulgence' (☎ 01872 573126; www.callestickfarm.co.uk). There is a café and ice cream parlour, and farm animals. Ice cream addicts should also track down ⓮ **Roskilly's** near St Keverne on the Lizard Peninsula (☎ 01326 280479; www.roskillys.co.uk) where wonderful ice cream is made on site from a Jersey herd there is a restaurant, craft workshops, milking demonstrations and calves to visit (p 159).

Cornwall's Arts & Crafts

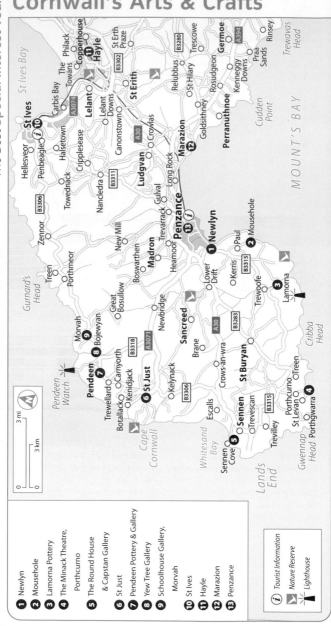

1 Newlyn
2 Mousehole
3 Lamorna Pottery
4 The Minack Theatre, Porthcurno
5 The Round House & Capstan Gallery
6 St Just
7 Pendeen Pottery & Gallery
8 Yew Tree Gallery
9 Schoolhouse Gallery, Morvah
10 St Ives
11 Hayle
12 Marazion
13 Penzance

i Tourist Information
Nature Reserve
Lighthouse

Artists have been drawn to Cornwall for well over a century by its amazing land- and seascapes and the incredible quality of the light, most dramatic in the far southwest. There are galleries all over the county, but many of the best are in West Penwith, especially in St Ives, an internationally famous artists' community since the early 20th century (p 46). Tourist Information Centres can supply information on local artists and galleries; some towns—St Ives and Penzance, for example—offer arts and crafts trails; Truro (p 136) and Falmouth (p 100) have leading galleries. Get hold of *The Galleries Guide for Cornwall & Devon*, published by Rainyday in Penzance (p 128). **START: Newlyn (1 mile/1½km) west of Penzance. Trip distance: 53 miles (85km). Trip length: 5 days.**

---

❶ Newlyn. Painters flocked to this leading fishing port in the late 19th century; many had previously studied in Brittany and were attracted to Cornwall's coastal landscapes for similar reasons. The Newlyn School of Artists was set up in 1899 by Stanhope and Elizabeth Forbes; Penzance's Penlee Gallery contains examples of their work (p 49).

Newlyn Art Gallery. Reopened in 2007 after major refurbishment, and run in conjunction with The Exchange, Penzance (p 49), this elegant waterfront gallery showcases national and international contemporary art, including much local work. *New Road, TR18 5PZ.* ☎ *01736 363715. www.newlynart gallery.co.uk. Free admission. Apr–end Oct Mon–Sat 10am–5pm, Nov–end Mar Tues–Sat 10am–5pm.*

Badcocks Gallery. Overlooking Newlyn's historic harbour, Badcocks is one of Cornwall's leading contemporary fine art galleries. It also displays sculpture, ceramics, jewellery and prints. *The Strand, TR18 5HW.* ☎ *01736 366159. www.badcocks gallery.co.uk. Free admission. Mon–Fri 10:30am–5:30pm, Sun 11am–5:30pm.*

Follow the coast road past the harbour to Mousehole. Distance: 1½ miles (2½km).

❷ Mousehole. The quaint fishing village of 'Mouzel' is a huddle of granite cottages around a tiny circular harbour. It was burned to the ground by the Spanish in 1595. The church contains a memorial to local resident Dolly Pentreath (died 1777), the last known native speaker of Cornish.The village is also associated with the story of the Mousehole Cat and Stargazey Pie.

The Tyler Gallery. Ornamental raku pottery (using a fire and smoke ceramic process), paintings, cards, prints and jewellery. *12 Brook Street TR19 6RD.* ☎ *01736 731109. www. tylergallery.co.uk. Free admission. Daily Mar–Dec 10am–6pm. Winter hours vary.*

Sandpiper Gallery. You can find a wide range of arts and crafts from Cornwall and beyond: furniture, pottery, wooden boats and fish, textiles, jewellery, stained glass and prints. *2 Carn Topna, TR19 6QE.* ☎ *01736 732441. www.sandpipergallery.co.uk. Free admission. Daily 10am–5:30pm.*

The Little Picture Gallery. This bright, friendly gallery displays representational, traditional and naïve works of art, plus prints, sculpture and wooden birds. *Mill Lane TR19 6RP.* ☎ *01736 732877. www.thelittle picturegallery.net. Free admission. Mon–Sat plus many Suns 11am–5pm.*

The Minack overlooks the bay at Porthcurno.

From the harbor, take the road signed to Lands End. In Paul, turn left (to Lands End); at junction in Sheffield, turn left onto the B3315 (Lands End); pottery is on the right. Distance: 2½ miles (4km).

③ Lamorna Pottery. The Pottery was set up in 1948 in an old milk factory; Bernard Leach (p 47) was a strong early influence. Glazed ware reflects the colours of the landscape: blues, greens, browns. There

Sennen Cove.

is a Garden Restaurant and accommodation. *Lamorna, Penzance TR19 6NY. ☎ 01736 810330. www.studio pottery.com. Free admission. Call for opening times.*

Continue along the B3315; at junction, turn left (to Lands End). After about 2 miles (3¼km), at Trethewey turn left (brown sign). Pass through Porthcurno and climb the cliff road. Distance 6½ miles (10½km).

④ The Minack Theatre, Porthcurno. *See p 35.*

Retrace your route to the B3315; turn left (to Lands End). After 3½ miles (5½km) turn right onto the A30; turn left to Sennen Cove; proceed to the harbour car park. Distance: 4¼ miles (6¾km).

⑤ The Round House & Capstan Gallery. Old cottages and boatsheds cluster round the working harbour of Lands End's nearest village (whose lifeboat crew is on permanent standby); the gallery building used to house the winch for hauling fishing boats up the slip. The gallery features local crafts, cards and jewellery for sale, plus work by artists inspired by West Penwith's dramatic landscapes. *Sennen Cove, Lands End TR19 7DF. ☎ 01736 871859.*

www.round-house.co.uk. Free admission. Daily 10am–6pm.

Retrace your route to the A30; turn left. Bear left onto the B3306 (to St Just). At T-junction, turn left onto the A3071 St Just. Distance: 5¼ miles (8½km).

6 St Just. Once an administrative centre for the mining industry, this town is now an artists' haven. Note Plain an Gwary (p 53) and have a bite at the very Cornish Kegen Teg ('Fair Kitchen') on Market Square.

Over the Moon Gallery. Supports new and emerging artists, and work from outside Cornwall. Ceramics, paintings, sculpture, glass, bronzes, wood and jewellery. *41 Fiore Street TR19 7LJ.* ☎ *01736 787052. www. overthemoongallery.co.uk. Free admission. Summer Mon–Sat 10:30am–5pm, winter Wed–Sat.*

Great Atlantic Gallery. Opened in 1966 as the Great Atlantic Map Works Gallery, it moved to its present site in 2007; displays a wide range of ceramics, paintings and prints, and has a

Looking out from the Capstan Gallery.

branch in Falmouth (p 100). *Bank Square TR19 7HH.* ☎ *01736 788911. www.greatatlantic.co.uk. Free admission. Mon–Sat 10:30am–5pm, Sun 2–5pm.*

Turn of the Tide Studio. This is the studio gallery of a painter specialising in the coastal landscape, festivals and people, and a painter/printmaker who draws on myth, symbolism and the natural environment. *35 Fore Street*

The Capstan Gallery.

Tate St Ives.

TR19 7LJ. ☎ 01736 787268. www.
hendersonsmith.co.uk. Free admission. Daily from 10am (most days).

Continue north on the B3306
towards St Ives through Pendeen.
Distance: 2¼ miles (3½km).

❼ Pendeen Pottery & Gallery.
This working pottery and gallery specialises in domestic ware, replica Victorian ware, still-life, landscape and
botanical paintings, Cornish artists
and potters. A jewellery workshop is
across the road. *Boscaswell Downs,
Pendeen TR19 7EW.* ☎ *01736
788070. Free admission. Summer
Mon–Sat 10am–5:30pm, winter Mon–
Fri 10am–5pm (times can vary).*

Continue north on the B3306
towards St Ives to pass the Yew
Tree Gallery (right). Distance:
1 mile (1½km).

❽ Yew Tree Gallery. Long-established gallery exhibiting contemporary and applied art by well-known
artists within and outside Cornwall;
also has sculpture gardens. Holds
frequent exhibitions of paintings,
prints, sculpture, ceramics, glass,
photo-graphy and jewellery. *Keigwin
Farmhouse, nr Morvah, Penzance
TR19 7TS.* ☎ *01736 786425. www.
yewtreegallery.com. Free admission.
Easter–end Oct Tues–Sat*

10:30am–5:30pm during exhibitions
(call for details).

Continue north on the B3306;
bear left off the road at Morvah.
Distance; ½ mile (¾km).

**❾ Schoolhouse Gallery, Mor-
vah.** This compact gallery, café and
community arts centre opened in
1999. It holds fortnightly exhibitions
of the work of local and regional
artists, plus story-telling, poetry,
music and film evenings. *Morvah,
Penzance TR20 8YT.* ☎ *01736
787808. www.morvah.com. Free
admission. Easter–end Oct Tues–
Sun & Bank Hol Mon 10am–5pm,
end Oct–Easter Thurs–Sun 11:30am–
4pm.*

Continue past the church; rejoin
the B3306, and turn left to St
Ives; follow signs for the Tate;
where the road bends sharply
left, head to the Barnoon car
park. Distance: 9½ miles (15¼km).

❿ St Ives. Set aside a couple of
days to explore this charming place.
By the 1870s the town was attracting
artists from all over the world, but it
was placed firmly on the art world's
map by Ben Nicholson and Barbara
Hepworth in the early 20th century
(p 133). Nicholson discovered local
artist Alfred Wallis (1855–1942)

whose primitive paintings are some of the best known from the St Ives School. St Ives contains a host of galleries, workshops and studios (small selection below), but the opening of the Tate St Ives in 1993 confirmed the town's position as the home of British post-war modernism.

Tate St Ives. This stunning building sits alongside the jumble of old fishermen's cottages and boatsheds behind Porthmeor beach. Patrick Heron, one of the best known post-war Cornish Artists, created the stained glass entrance window at Tate St Ives. *See p 133.*

Barbara Hepworth Museum & Sculpture Garden. One of Britain's most important 20th-century artists lived here from 1949 until her death in 1975; together the subtropical garden (modernist sculptures), studio and house form a small museum of her work. *Barnoon Hill TR26 1TG. Contact details and opening times as for Tate St Ives. Adult £4.65, child (under 18) free, concessions £2.70.*

The Leach Pottery. Established in 1920 by Bernard Leach and Japanese potter Shoji Hamada, this became a centre of excellence. After extensive refurbishment in March 2008, the site now contains the historic pottery

buildings and museum, studio and training facilities, shop and a selling gallery; it puts on regular exhibitions of work by local, national and international potters. *Higher Stennack TR26 2HE.* ☎ *01736 799703. www.leachpottery.com. Free admission but a charge for entry to old workshop and museum. Mar–Sept Mon–Sat 10am–5pm 9 Sun 11am–4pm), Oct–Feb Tues–Sat 10am–4pm.*

St Ives Society of Artists & Mariners. Founded in 1927, the Society now exhibits mainly figurative work in a former mariners' church in Norway Square. *Norway Square TR26 1TG.* ☎ *01736 795582. www.stisa.co.uk. Free admission. Mid-Mar–Oct Mon–Sat 10:30am–5:30pm (Whitsun–end Sept Sun pm); Dec Tues Sat 10:30am–4:30pm. Open Bank Hol Sun/Mon.*

Retrace your route to the B3306 out of St Ives. After 1 mile (1½km), turn left (the B3311 signed to Penzance), and then left signed Redruth/Hayle. At the Lelant roundabout turn right and almost immediately left onto the B3301 (to Hayle). In Hayle, turn right for car park. Distance: 7 miles (11¼km).

⑪ Hayle. The Hayle estuary is an internationally significant Royal Society for the Protection of Birds

Hepworth Garden at St Ives.

Exhibits on display in the Bernard Leach Pottery Museum.

reserve; migrant birds gather in vast numbers in spring and autumn. By the 1850s the town was the greatest industrial port in Cornwall; only the abandoned wharves remain today.

Hayle Gallery. This gallery specialises in 19th- and 20th-century Cornish art, with a good selection from the St Ives and Newlyn Schools. *22 Penpol Terrace TR27 4BQ.* ☎ *01736 758465. www.hayle gallery.co.uk. Free admission. Mon–Fri 9am–5:30pm, Sat 9:30am–2pm.*

Foundry Gallery. On the upper floor of an old Wesleyan chapel are several artists' studios and workshops, plus gallery and exhibition space. There is a painter, photographer, print maker, silver jewellery maker and ceramic studio. Original works from late 19th-century to contemporary artists. *Unit 12, Pratts Market, Chapel Terrace TR27 4AB.* ☎ *01736 752787. www.foundrygallery.co.uk. Free admission. Mon–Sat 9am–5pm.*

Retrace your route to the B3301 back towards St Ives; take the A30 (Penzance). After about 5 miles (8km), at Newtown roundabout take second left (to Marazion); turn next left. Distance: 7½ miles (12km).

⑫ Marazion. This town is Cornwall's oldest charter town (dating from 1257) and was Mount's Bay's main port until Penzance took over in the 16th century. Try the excellent Cornish pasties from Philps Bakery (also in Hayle).

Out of the Blue. Colourful little gallery on Marazion's historic square: crafts are on lower floor, such as copperware, ceramics, stained glass, driftwood, jewellery, prints and cards. The upper gallery showcases local artists; regular exhibitions. *The Square TR17 0AP.* ☎ *01736 719019. www.out-of-the-blue-gallery.co.uk. Free admission. Summer Mon–Fri 10:30am–5:30pm (from midday Sun), winter Mon–Fri 11am–4pm (Sun 2–4pm) (times can vary).*

Market House Gallery. Marazion's largest gallery, in a Georgian building, shows acclaimed 20th-century Cornish artists, especially post-war work, plus sculpture, glassware, studio and retro pottery, current and out-of-print books: regular exhibitions. *Market Square TR17 0AR.* ☎ *01736 710252. www.markethousegallery.co.uk. Free admission. Daily midday–5:30pm.*

Seagrove Gallery. Displaying a wide range of arts and crafts, including 'wearable' art from the UK's top makers, this gallery also has a tea garden overlooking St Michael's Mount. *The Square TR17 0AR.* ☎ *01736 710732.*

Free admission. Summer daily 10:30am–6pm, winter Wed–Sun 11am–4:30pm.

Avalon Art. Just opposite the St Michael's Mount causeway, this galley features high-quality paintings (abstract, naïve, seascapes, landscapes), pottery, jewellery and work from prominent Cornish-based artists. *West End R17 0EL.* ☎ *01736 710161. Free admission. Summer daily 10:30am–5:30pm, winter Mon–Sat 11am–4:30pm.*

Retrace your route out of Marazion to the A30; turn left (to Penzance). After 2½ miles (4km) at the Branwell Lane roundabout keep straight ahead (to town centre) and harbour car park. Distance: 3¼ miles (5¼km).

⑬ Penzance. Penzance has galleries and studios galore (see also p 128) and so take time to explore: just a handful are mentioned below.

Penlee House Gallery & Museum. 'The artistic heart of West Cornwall's heritage' has a gallery, museum, café and shop plus year-round exhibitions, including work by the Newlyn and Lamorna artists (1880–1900). *Morrab Road TR18 4HE.* ☎ *01736 363625. www.penleehouse.org.uk. Adult £3, child (under 18) free, concessions £2. Easter–end Sept Mon–Sat 10am–5pm, Oct–Easter 10:30am–4pm.*

Mural at Penzance station.

The Exchange. This important new gallery in the old telephone exchange opened in July 2007, in association with the Newlyn Art Gallery (p 43); it displays top-quality national and international contemporary art. *Princes Street TR18 2NL.* ☎ *01736 363715. www.theexchangegallery. co.uk. Free admission. from 1 Mar–end Oct Mon–Sat 10am–5pm, 1 Nov–end Feb Tues–Sat.*

Goldfish. Cutting-edge gallery, specialising in contemporary mixed-media fine art: permanent gallery and exhibitions. *56 Chapel Street TR18 4 AE.* ☎ *01736 360573. www. goldfishfineart.co.uk. Free admission. Mon–Sat 10am–5pm.*

The Art Pass

The Art Pass allows unlimited access to six outstanding venues across west Cornwall: Tate St Ives, Barbara Hepworth Museum and Sculpture Garden, Leach Pottery (all in St Ives), Penlee House Gallery & Museum and The Exchange (Penzance), and Newlyn Art Gallery. It costs £12 (concessions £7) for a 7-day period, and is available at all the participating galleries and museums. Cardholders receive a 10% discount in the shops at the Newlyn Art Gallery and The Exchange (which don't charge for entrance).

Ancient Cornwall

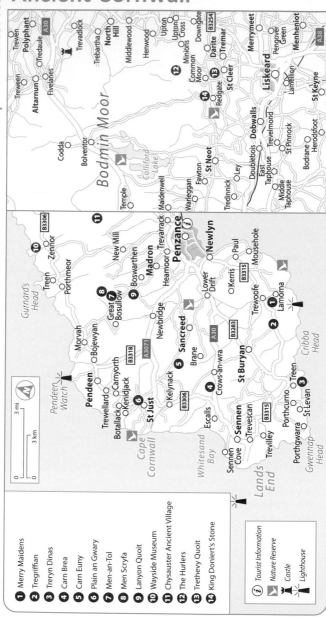

1 Merry Maidens
2 Tregriffian
3 Treryn Dinas
4 Carn Brea
5 Carn Euny
6 Plain an Gwary
7 Men-an-Tol
8 Men Scryfa
9 Lanyon Quoit
10 Wayside Museum
11 Chysauster Ancient Village
12 The Hurlers
13 Trethevy Quoit
14 King Doniert's Stone

(i) Tourist Information
Nature Reserve
Castle
Lighthouse

When it comes to historic sites, West Penwith holds all the aces. The greatest concentration of prehistoric monuments anywhere in Cornwall is found on its windswept moors, although Bodmin Moor also has many interesting antiquities (p 94). Some sites lie conveniently near the roadside; others (including the ones in this tour) involve a short walk. Western Cornwall and the Isles of Scilly are the only places in Britain where *fogous* (chambered underground passages, dating from late Iron Age or Romano-British times) have been found. Their exact purpose is still obscure.

START: **Penzance. Trip distance: 36 miles (58km). Trip length: 2 days.**

The Merry Maidens stone circle.

From Penzance, follow the signs for Newlyn along the seafront. In Newlyn, keep ahead on the B3315 (to Lamorna). After 3¾ miles (6km) stop in layby on the left. Distance: 4¾ miles (7½km).

❶ ★★ **Merry Maidens.** The story goes that this stone circle of 19 dressed granite blocks represents the petrified remains of a group of local lasses, turned to stone for dancing on the Sabbath. The monument dates from the Bronze Age and is one of few 'true' (perfectly circular) stone circles in Cornwall. It forms part of an extensive ceremonial landscape. Two single standing stones, known as the Pipers, stand in a field to the north-east, on the opposite side of the road. *St Buryan.* ⏲ *20 min.*

❷ ★★ **Tregriffian.** A short distance west of the Merry Maidens, this chambered tomb can be seen by the roadside. The northern half of the tomb was chopped off when the road was constructed, but there is still enough left to give a good

impression of what the complete structure would have looked like. It was built during the Neolithic period (3000–2000 B.C.), and possibly remodelled during the Bronze Age. The original cup-marked entrance stone is in Truro Museum, but a replica is in situ. *St Buryan.* ⏲ *10 min.*

Tregriffian chambered tomb.

Men-an-Tol.

Continue along the B3315 (note the stone crosses along road-side). At the T-junction, turn left; after ¾ mile (1¼km) turn left into Treen and head for the car park. Distance: 3¼ miles (5¼km).

3 ★★ Treryn Dinas. Walk left out of the car park, and then left again, following a well-signed track across arable fields to the South West Coast Path and Treryn Dinas (20 minutes). Not much survives of this Iron Age cliff castle (800 B.C.–A.D. 43), but it is worth a visit for its breathtaking location above the bay and views towards the Minack Theatre (p 35). The landward side is defended by three pairs of ramparts and ditches. Cliff castles were built on similar promontories all around the Cornish coast, but they are thought to have fallen out of use when the Romans invaded Britain. *Treen.* ⏱ *1½ hr.*

Retrace your route to the B3315; turn right and follow the B3283 (to St Buryan). In St Buryan, turn left by the church, signed to St Just. Turn left on the A30 (to Lands End). After ¼ mile (½km), turn right in Crows-an-wra. The car park is on the left. Distance: 5 miles (8km).

4 ★ Carn Brea. This parking area gives access to the breezy site of Carn Brea, which crowns mainland Britain's most westerly hill (657ft/200m high). This Bronze Age summit cairn (chambered tomb) is of a kind only found in Cornwall and the Isles of Scilly. In medieval times there was a hermitage and chapel on the hill-top, and a beacon is still lit here every midsummer eve by fishermen from St Just. There are wonderful views from the top. *Crows-an-wra.* ⏱ *1 hr.*

5 ★★★ Carn Euny. A slightly longer walk leads to an even more impressive site. Cross the road from the car park and follow the bridle-path (keeping straight on through a pair of stone gateposts). After about 1 mile (1½km) you will spot a small well by the path; turn right at the next track, then left at the sign to Carn Euny. The substantial remains of this Roman-British village and associated field systems (built on top of an Iron Age site) were first excavated in the 1860s. The site was occupied between 550 B.C. and A.D. 400. The courtyard houses are again of a type unique in West Penwith and the Isles of Scilly (see **11** Chysauster

Lanyon Quoit.

The Wayside Museum, Zennor.

Ancient Village on p 54). They were built with turf and wattle walls, daubed with clay and roofed with thatch or turf. Don't miss the fogou (the Cornish word for 'cave'), which looks like a human-made cave. *Sancreed.* 🕑 *2 hr.*

From the car park, turn left. Turn right onto the B3306; turn left onto the A3071 (to St Just). Turn right for car park. Distance: 2¾ miles (4½km).

6 ★ Plain an Gwary. Near the car park is a large embanked grassy area known as Plain an Gwary ('playing place'), a medieval amphitheatre where miracle plays in the Cornish language were performed; for centuries afterwards it was used as a meeting place. Though not especially impressive today, this site is of historic importance. These monuments are peculiar to Cornwall, and seem to have been constructed in places where the Cornish language survived in late medieval times. When the site was first recorded in the mid-18th century, it had six tiers of stone steps built into the encircling bank. *St Just.* 🕑 *10 min.*

Leave the car park; at Market Square turn left onto the B3306. After just over 4 miles (6½km), take the first right turn after Morvah (Madron); turn right at the T-junction. Stop in layby opposite first house on right. Distance: 5½ miles (8¾km).

7 ★★ Men-an-Tol. Less than a mile from the parking area, a signed footpath leads to the impressive Bronze Age monument of Men-an-Tol ('holed stone'), a large rock with a hole big enough for a child to pass through. Folk tradition endowed this stone with magical healing powers (for example, for rickets), but its original prehistoric significance is unknown. Such stones are very rare in Cornwall. A little farther up the main track, in a field to the left, stands the inscribed stone.

8 Men Scryfa. This monument probably dates from the Bronze Age, but the inscription is thought to be Celtic, possibly from the 5th or 6th century AD. *Madron.* 🕑 *1 hr.*

Continue in the same direction towards Madron; look for the small parking area on right. Distance: ¾ mile (1¼km).

House at Chysauster village.

The Hurlers stone circles.

⑨ ★★ Lanyon Quoit.

This is a megalithic chambered tomb, used for communal burial in the Neolithic period. Such tombs are known as quoits or dolmens in Celtic areas, and the huge stones would originally have been partially covered with earth. Lanyon Quoit is thought to date from around 2000 B.C. It collapsed in 1815 and was rebuilt; the original structure would have stood higher than it does today. *Madron.* ⏱ *20 min.*

Retrace your route to the B3306; turn right (towards St Ives). After about 4 miles (6½km), turn left into Zennor. Distance: 6 miles (9½km).

⑩ ★★★ Wayside Museum.

The items in this extraordinary little museum all originate in West Penwith. In 1924 an army colonel called Freddie Hirst retired from India to Zennor and started collecting archaeological artefacts from the surrounding moor. Today this glorious treasure trove of diverse and densely packed exhibits casts light on many aspects of life in this southwesterly corner of Cornwall from 3000 B.C. to the 1950s. It occupies a series of small, interlinked rooms, and includes a 16th-century miller's cottage and a watermill. Treat yourself to a delicious Moomaid ice cream from the gift shop, made locally in Zennor. ⏱ *2 hr. Zennor TR26 3DA.* ☎ *01736 796945. Adult £3.75, child (ages 2–16) £2.25, family £11. Apr and Oct Sun–Fri 11am–5pm, May–end Sept Sun–Fri 10:30am–5:30pm.*

Head towards the church, and then turn right; turn right onto the B3306. Take the first left (to Penzance). At the junction, turn left; after 1 mile (1½km) turn left signed to Chysauster. Distance: 4½ miles (7¼km).

⑪ ★★★ Chysauster Ancient Village.

There is little evidence that the Romans made much impact on Cornwall; their main base in south-western Britain was Isca Dumnoniorum (Exeter) in Devon. During the period of Roman occupation (1st–4th centuries) Chysauster was inhabited by a farming community, who lived in stone-built 'courtyard' houses, unusually arranged along a 'street'. Houses 4 and 6 are the best preserved (excellent interpretation boards scattered round the site give

Megalithic Trethevy Quoit.

King Doniert's stone.

a clear picture of the room plans). You can even see the remains of hearths and garden terraces. Don't miss the on-site fogou. ⏱ *1½ hr. Nr Gulval TR20 8XA.* ☎ *07831 757934. www.english-heritage.org.uk. Adult £3, child (ages 5–15) £1.50, concessions £2.60; English Heritage members free. Daily 1 Apr–end Sept 10am–5pm, during Oct 10am–4pm.*

Turn right from the car park; turn right at Badgers Cross onto the B3311. Follow the signs to Penzance. Distance: 3½ miles (5½km).

⓬ **The Hurlers.** Dating from the Bronze Age (c. 1500 B.C.), the Hurlers stands on Minions Moor near the Heritage Centre (p 19). It consists of a unique formation of three aligned rings of standing stones. Legend has it that the Hurlers (rather like the Merry Maidens—see ❶ above) represent men changed to stone as a punishment for the sin of 'hurling' the ball on a Sunday. *Minions.* ⏱ *20 min.*

⓭ **Trethevy Quoit.** This huge, well-preserved, early Neolithic quoit (a chambered tomb or portal dolmen) is undeniably impressive. It stands on a small hillock in a field and consists of seven uprights (one of which has fallen) supporting a 12ft (3½m) capstone. Probably erected somewhere between 3700 and 3300 B.C., this twin-chambered structure dates from the time of the first settled farming in the area. It would originally have been partially covered with earth. No bones survive in Cornish quoits due to the acid soil. A hole in the stone slab on the western side is possibly a 'midsummer' or 'merriment' hole. In times gone by, young men would make these holes, fill them with explosives and detonate them as a demonstration of love for their sweethearts. *St Cleer, Liskeard.* ⏱ *20 min.*

⓮ **King Doniert's Stone.** Two granite cross bases stand in an enclosure by the B3254 1 mile (1½km) northwest of St Cleer. Latin inscriptions ask for prayers for an early Cornish king called Doniert (or Durngarth) who drowned in the River Fowey in A.D. 875. *St Cleer, Liskeard.* ⏱ *20 min.*

The Antiquities of Bodmin Moor

Bodmin Moor, designated as an Area of Outstanding Beauty, is peppered with prehistoric monuments. Three significant sites can be found in the St Cleer/Minions area on the southeastern edge of the moor.

Cornwall's Castles & Historic Houses

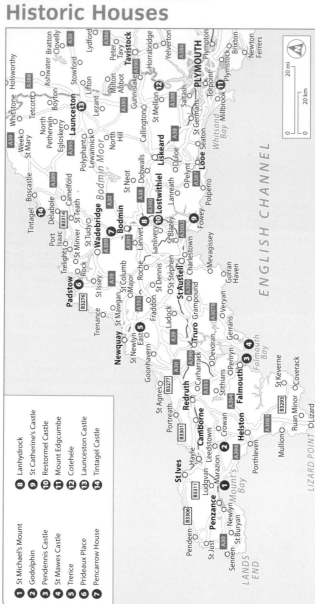

1 St Michael's Mount
2 Godolphin
3 Pendennis Castle
4 St Mawes Castle
5 Trerice
6 Prideaux Place
7 Pencarrow House
8 Lanhydrock
9 St Catherine's Castle
10 Restormel Castle
11 Mount Edgcumbe
12 Cotehele
13 Launceston Castle
14 Tintagel Castle

From the impressive 13th-century remains of Launceston Castle to Lanhydrock, one of the country's most impressive examples of Victorian domestic architecture, Cornwall is blessed with a great variety of castles and historic houses from medieval to Victorian times. Some have been owned by the same family for centuries; others are under the care of English Heritage or the National Trust. START: **St Michael's Mount (Marazion, 2 miles/3¼km west of Penzance). Trip distance: 208 miles (333km). Trip length: 4–5 days.**

① ★★★ kids St Michael's Mount.

The romantic setting of this fortified priory perched on a rocky tidal island just off Marazion exerts a magnetic pull on the imagination. A visit here is not to be missed, at least once in a lifetime. The oldest buildings date from Norman times, when Benedictine monks recreated an abbey, based on the design of Mont-St-Michel across the Channel, and dedicated it to the same archangelic patron. Henry VIII incorporated the site into his chain of coastal defences in the 16th century. The St Aubyn family, who still live here, became owners after the English Civil War, turning the castle into a luxurious mansion. Today the property is in the care of the NT. Getting to the island is quite an adventure: at low tide you can walk across the stone causeway; otherwise, you must take a boat. Never try to beat the tides, which race in very swiftly. St Michael's Mount is not a place for the infirm or for pushchairs: there's a long, rocky climb up the castle, and many steps. Dogs aren't allowed. ⏱ *4 hr; access on foot at low tide, by boat at high; crowded in holiday season. Marazion, nr Penzance TR17 0EF. ☎ 01736 710507/710265 (tide and ferry). www.stmichaelsmount.co.uk & www.nationaltrust.org.uk. Castle & garden: adult £8.10, child (ages 5–16) £3.30, family (2 adults) £20, family (1 adult) £11.90. NT members free. 29 Mar–30 Jun, 1 Sept–1 Nov 10:30am–5pm (closed Sat), 1 Jul–31 Aug 10:30am–5:30pm (closed Sat).*

From St Michael's Mount, head east through Marazion towards the A394. At the roundabout, go straight ahead on the B3280 for Leedstown and Godolphin (brown sign). Turn right at Townshend (Goldophin 1 mile/1½km). Distance: 6 miles (9½km).

② ★★★ Godolphin.

This grand family seat is in a time-warp, with the house and garden virtually

St Michael's Mount.

Godolphin's inner courtyard.

all year; garden end Mar–1 Nov
Mon, Tues, Wed, Sat & Sun 10am–
5pm; house daily late Apr–late Sept
11am–5pm.

Turn right; then left to join the
B3302 and head for Helston. Turn
left onto the A394 to Helston;
pick up signs for Falmouth (the
A394). At the Treliever roundabout, turn right; follow the A39
into Falmouth to pick up brown
signs. Turn right onto the 'scenic
route'. Distance: 21 miles
(33½km).

③ ★★ kids Pendennis Castle.
In the mid-16th century Henry VIII
constructed a string of artillery forts
along England's southern shores to
ward off attacks by Spain and
France. Pendennis Castle in an
excellent defensive position on Pendennis Head. It and St Mawes Castle
(see 4 below) were built to protect
the great natural harbour of the Carrick Roads. Pendennis was further
fortified in the 16th century (under
Elizabeth I) against the threat of
Spanish attack by the construction
of huge ramparts and bastions.
English Heritage runs a varied programme of special activities for
children during holiday periods.
🕐 2 hr; huge site so rarely crowded.
Falmouth TR11 4LP. ☎ 01326
312300. www.english-heritage.org.
uk. Adult £5.70, child (ages 5–15)
£2.90, family £14.30, concessions
£4.80. English Heritage members
free. Daily Apr–Jun & Sep 10am–
5pm, Jul–Aug 10am–6pm, Oct–Mar
10am–4pm.

unchanged since the early 18th century. The Godolphin family first
came to prominence in the 12th and
13th centuries. Their wealth was
largely derived through mining, land
expansion and calculated mar-
riages; by Tudor times they were
one of Cornwall's most influential
families. Their home was the largest
and grandest house in 17th-century
Cornwall, but after they moved to
London in the early 18th century
Godolphin fell into neglect until it
was purchased by the Schofield
family in 1937. Acquired by the NT
in 2000, the estate attracted
250,000 visitors during its first
opening season. The garden is of
great historical importance, a
unique survival of medieval horticultural style. 🕐 3 hr; popular site;
access restricted to certain areas.
Godolphin Cross, Helston TR13 9RE.
☎ 01736 762479. www.national
trust.org.uk. Adult £2.70, child (ages
5–16) £1.35. House & garden: adult
£3.70, child (ages 5–16) £1.85, family
(2 adults) £9.25, family (1 adult)
£5.50. NT members free. Estate open

Follow the A39 out of Falmouth
via Truro, and then, keeping on
the A39, follow the signs for Bodmin as far as the A30. Turn right
onto the A30; turn left onto the
A3058 (brown sign). At Kestle
Mill, turn right for just under 1
mile (1½km). Distance: 25½ miles
(41km).

View from St Anthony Head to St Mawes Castle.

4 ★★ St Mawes Castle. This clover-shaped structure is one of the least altered and best preserved of Henry's coastal fortifications, and the most elaborately decorated. The castle was captured without resistance by Parliamentary forces in 1646. It has superb views of the Carrick Roads from the keep. ⊕ *1 hr. Roseland Peninsula TR2 5DE.* ☎ *01326 270526. www.english-heritage.co.uk. Adult £4, child (ages 5–15) £2, concessions £3.40. English Heritage members free. Apr–Jun & Sep Sun–Fri 10am–5pm, Jul–Aug 10am–6pm, daily Oct 10am–4pm, Nov–end Mar Fri–Mon 10am–4pm.*

5 ★★★ Trerice. This Elizabethan manor is one of Cornwall's finest houses, little changed since its construction in 1572 and home to the Royalist Civil War hero, John Arundell. (The gabled, mullioned building was left standing empty for long periods by absentee owners.) It lies tucked away in gentle Cornish countryside down narrow country lanes. ⊕ *3 hr. Kestle Mill, Nr Newquay TR8 4PG.* ☎ *01637 875404. www. nationaltrust.org.uk. Adult £7, child (ages 5–16) £3.50, family (2 adults)* *£17.50, family (1 adult) £10.50. NT members free. House & shop daily 28 Feb–1 Nov (but closed Fri) 11am–5pm; garden and tearoom: daily 28 Feb–1 Nov 10:30am–5pm (also closed Fri).*

Return to Kestle Mill; turn left onto the A3058 to Newquay. Keep ahead at the Quintrell Downs roundabout (the A3058 to Porth). Turn right at mini-roundabout after 3¼ miles (5¼km) onto the B3276 to Padstow. Stay on the B3276 (bear right at Watergate Bay). Pass through St Merryn after 11½ miles (18½km); after Windmill bear left towards Padstow. Turn left to Prideaux Place. Distance: 17 miles (27½km).

6 ★★ Prideaux Place. This house has been the seat of the Prideaux family since Elizabethan times. The Elizabethan exterior set in a deer park is handsome enough, but the interior is splendid too, with sumptuous porcelain and plasterwork in the Strawberry Hill Gothick style. It was the first house in Cornwall to have electricity. Watch out for ghosts: highwaymen, murdered monks and a dog! The ancient

Prideaux Place, Padstow.

gardens have been extensively restored over recent years. 🕑 *2 hr. Padstow PL28 8RP.* ☎ *01841 532411. www.prideauxplace.co.uk. Call for admission fees. House: Sun–Thurs 1:30–4pm; grounds mid-May–early Oct & Easter Sun 12:30pm–5pm.*

Rejoin the A389; turn left. Turn left onto the A389 Wadebridge, and then the A39 Bude/Bodmin. At roundabout, take the A39 towards Bodmin (brown sign). At Washaway, follow brown signs left (Old School Lane). Distance: 12½ miles (20km).

❼ ★★ kids Pencarrow House. This lovely Georgian house in 50 acres (20 hectares) of landscaped gardens has been owned by the Molesworth-St Aubyns for 500 years. John Molesworth originally moved here in the 16th century as auditor for the Duchy of Cornwall and Queen Elizabeth I. The gardens, originally laid out in the 19th century and extensively restored after World War II, include magnificent rhododendrons and a beautiful sunken Italian garden. One of the family dogs may help conduct a guided tour. 🕑 *3 hr; extensive grounds so unlikely to be crowded. Bodmin, PL30 3AG.* ☎ *01208 841369.*

www.pencarrow.co.uk. House & garden tour: adult £8.50, child (under 17) £4; garden only: adult £4, child under 17 £1. House: Apr–end Sept Sun–Thurs 11am–5pm; gardens: Mar–end Oct 9:30am–5:30pm.

Return to the A389 and turn left (towards Bodmin). Follow the signs left to the town centre (A38/A30). At the next round-about, turn left (to Lanhydrock/Liskeard). Pick up brown signs; keep ahead over next round-about on the A389. At the next roundabout, turn left onto the A38 Plymouth; at the next, turn right (to Lostwithiel). Turn left as signposted. Distance: 16½ miles (10½km).

❽ ★★ Lanhydrock. One of the most impressive 19th-century houses in England, lavishly rebuilt on the site of an earlier building. Only the original 17th-century gatehouse and north wing survived a fire in 1881. Fifty rooms are open to visitors, and so allow time for a proper exploration. Footpaths follow the Fowey Valley to Restormel Castle outside Lostwithiel (see ❾ below). The beautiful gardens containing fine shrubs and specimen trees were laid out in Victorian times. 🕑 *5 hr; huge site, rarely crowded but house can be* *busy in holiday times. Bodmin PL30 5AD.* ☎ *01208 265950 www.national trust.org.uk. Adult £10.40, child (ages 5–16) £5.20, family (2 adults) £26, family (1 adult) £15.60. 28 Feb–1 Aug & 1 Sept 1–Nov (not Mon) 11am–5:30pm; daily during Aug 11am–5:30pm. NT members free.*

Retrace your route; turn left at first junction. At the roundabout, turn left onto the B3268 to Lostwithiel. After 3½ miles (5½km), turn right onto the A390 to St Austell and then left onto the B3269 to Fowey. At the roundabout, keep ahead (Fowey 1 mile/1½km). Follow signs for Readymoney, and then brown signs for St Catherine's Castle. Distance: 10 miles (16km). Follow signed footpath to Readymoney Cove, then right on coast path, and then left and left again (15 min).

9 ★ **St Catherine's Castle.** This two-storey artillery fort was built in the 1530s, and later incorporated into Henry VIII's coastal defences. One of the main reasons for a visit is to enjoy extensive views over Fowey and Polruan on the opposite side of the estuary. The fort housed anti-aircraft guns in World War II to protect craft massing in the estuary

St Catherine's Castle, Fowey.

before the D-Day invasion on 6 June 1944. Access is via a short (sometimes slippery) and uneven walk. ⏲ *30 min; plus 15-min walk from the nearest parking area. Fowey PL23 1ET. www.english-heritage.co.uk. Free admission. Open all year.*

Follow the 'outbound traffic' signs to the A390 after 6 miles (9½km). Turn right (to Lostwithiel) and then left (brown signs) in town. Distance: 8½ miles (13¾km).

10 ★★★ **kids** **Restormel Castle.** Restormel both looks and feels like a real castle where you can walk around the top of the ramparts (watch out for slippery steps). The substantial ruins sit on a bluff high above the River Fowey. This is the best-preserved motte-and-bailey—an enditched mound (usually artificial), that forms the castle's strongpoint, surrounded by bailey or courtyard—castle in Cornwall. It originally dates from Norman times and was extensively refurbished in the 13th century by Edmund, Earl of Cornwall, when Lostwithiel was the capital of Cornwall (p 117). ⏲ *1 hr; rarely crowded. Lostwithiel PL22 0EE.* ☎ *01208 872687. www.english-heritage.co.uk. Adult £3, child (ages 5–15) £1.50, concessions £2.60.*

The keep at Restormel Castle.

Daily Apr–Jun & Sep 10am–5pm, Jul–Aug 10am–6pm, Oct 10am–4pm. EH members free.

Return to the A390; turn left to Liskeard. Join the A38 at Dobwalls towards Plymouth. At the Trerulefoot roundabout (16 miles/25½km), turn right onto the A374 to Torpoint (brown signs). Turn right after 22½ miles (36km). Follow signs through Crafthole;

Fort Picklecombe, Mount Edgcumbe.

join the B3247 through Millbrook. Eventually find Mount Edgcumbe on the right (keep downhill if aiming for lower country park car park). Distance: 38½ miles (61km).

⑪ ★★ kids Mount Edgcumbe. The former home of the Earls of Edgcumbe was built between 1547 and 1553. The house was damaged during World War II and has been restored. A major attraction is the Country Park and gardens: the 18th-century Earl's Garden near the house and the formal gardens in the lower park, in English, French and Italian styles. There is also an American and a New Zealand-styled garden. ⏱ 5 hr (if exploring country park as well); large site so never crowded. Cremyll, Torpoint PL10 1HZ. ☎ 01752 822236. www.mount edgcumbe.gov.uk. Adult £6, child (under 16) £3.50, family £12.50, concessions £5. Apr–end Sept Sun–Thurs 11am–4:30pm.

Follow the B3247/A374 back to Trerulefoot. Turn right onto the A38 towards Plymouth. After 15½ miles (25km) turn left, signed Callington, to join the A388; turn left (brown sign). Turn right at Viverdon Down, follow signs. Distance: 23 miles (37km).

⑫ ★★★ **kids** **Cotehele.** Step back to the 15th century. Small dark rooms, tapestries, unlit staircases—there's no electricity—create a homely atmosphere. The house is little changed since it was built between 1485 and 1539 by the Edgcumbe family (see ⑩ above), and has spent much of its life shut up while the Edgcumbes stayed at Mount Edgcumbe. Allow time to explore the beautiful gardens, which run downhill to the Tamar, and 19th-century Cotehele Quay with its warehouses and limekilns and, a short walk away, a working flour mill. ⏱ *5 hr; popular site but extensive grounds, quay and mill. St Dominick, nr Saltash PL12 6TA.* ☎ *01579 351346. www.nationaltrust.org.uk. Adult £9.20, child (ages 5–16) £4.60, family (2 adults) £23, family (1 adult) £13.80. NT members free. Daily mid-Mar–1 Nov 11am–4:30pm (closed Fri, end Feb–early Mar Sat 11am–4pm, garden open all year 10am–dusk.*

Mount Edgcumbe.

Return to Viverdon Down (3 miles/4¾km). Turn right onto the A388 to Callington/Launceston. After 5½ miles (8¾km) reach Callington; stay on the A388 signed Launceston for a farther 11 miles (17¾km). Distance: 19½ miles (15¼km).

⑬ ★★ **kids** **Launceston Castle.** Launceston was walled in the 12th century; most of what remains of the castle today (built soon after the Norman Conquest) dates from the 13th century when it was remodelled under Richard, Earl of Cornwall. He ordered the construction of the unusual keep—a round tower built on a natural mound, inside an earlier shell keep. The castle has never seen active service, but changed hands five times during the English Civil War. A display in the entrance building tells the story of the castle over the last 1,000 years.

St Mawes Castle

One of Henry VIII's prettiest coastal fortifications is St Mawes Castle guarding the Carrick Roads. There are two ways to reach it: by pedestrian ferry from Falmouth's Prince of Wales Pier (25 minutes) or by car on the King Harry Ferry (☎ 01872 862312; www.kingharryscornwall.co.uk), signed from Carnon Downs (the A39) and then follow the signs for St Mawes (18½ miles/29km from Falmouth). After your visit, pick up the directions to Trerice above.

Tintagel, seen from the South West Coast Path.

🕐 *1½ hr; large site, rarely crowded. Launceston PL15 7DR.* ☎ *01566 772365. www.englishheritage.org. uk. Adult £3, child (ages 5–15) £1.50, concessions £2.60. EH members free. Daily Apr–Jun & Sept, 10am–5pm, Jul–Aug 10am–6pm, Oct 10am–4pm.*

Return to the A30 and head west (towards Bodmin). After 3 miles (4¾km) take the A395 (towards North Cornwall). Turn left onto the A39 Wadebridge, and then right on the B3314 Tintagel. Keep straight over at Camelford Station; turn right onto the B3263. Follow the brown signs left in Tintagel for car parks. Distance: 19½ miles (31¼km). Follow footpath signs for ½ mile (¾km) to the castle entrance; Land Rover service for infirm; 100+ steep steps onto the island.

⑭ ★★★ kids Tintagel Castle.
Tintagel's Arthurian associations are much exploited locally, but the castle itself couldn't seem less commercialised. The cliff-top setting is truly spectacular; dramatic ruins teeter on a rugged headland linked by a long flight of steps to an island, where more ruinous medieval fortifications can be explored. Evidence of occupation dates from the 5th and 6th centuries, when Tintagel may have been a trading settlement of Celtic kings. 🕐 *4 hr; very popular site but access to the island is unsuitable for elderly and infirm. Tintagel PL34 0HE.* ☎ *01840 770328. www.nationaltrust.org.uk. Adult £4.90, child (ages 5–15) £2.50, family £12:30, concessions £4.20. EH members free. Daily Apr–end Sept 10am–6pm, Oct 10am–5pm, Nov– end Mar 10am–4pm.* ●

Cornwall's Best **Beaches**

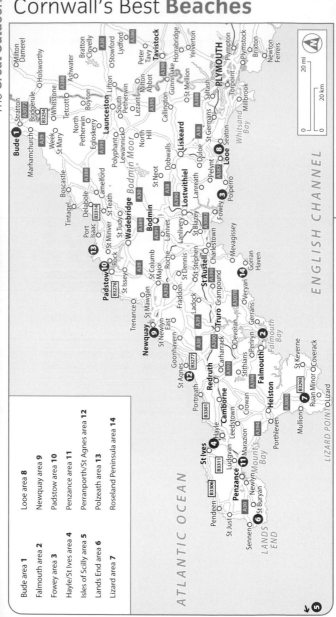

Previous page: Gull Rocks in Holywell Bay.

Cornwall has over 500 miles (805km) of coastline, with more than 300 beaches to suit all tastes. Family-friendly ones promise soft sand, shallow seas and enticing rock pools, plus parking, ice cream and deckchairs conveniently on hand. The north coast is famed for its huge, glamorous surfing beaches with hire shops and trendy cafés. Keen walkers and connoisseurs of coastal scenery have an enviable choice of quiet, sheltered coves accessible only via a challenging walk from the nearest parking spot. Some of Cornwall's main coastal settlements, such as Bude, Newquay, St Ives, Falmouth and East Looe, have lovely beaches right in the heart of town, with many offering watersports such as windsurfing or kayaking. Visit www.cornwall beachguide.co.uk for details and www.cornwall-beaches.co.uk; links list Blue Flag beaches in Cornwall that are recognised for good water quality and facilities. If you're a novice swimmer, only use beaches with lifeguard cover (indicated by a red-and-yellow flag). A red flag means swimming is forbidden; take a look at www.goodbeachguide.co.uk.

Bude area

Crackington Haven   Large, sand-and-pebble beach with a stream, rock pools and high cliffs (unstable but eye-catching folded rocks): surfing, car park, café.

Crooklets Beach   Central, sandy, popular beach: surfing, car park, café.

Duckpool Beach   A small, quiet, pebbly bay on National Trust (NT) land with stream and sand at low tide: limited parking, no facilities.

Summerleaze Beach   Central resort beach near sea lock and canal museum, sandy, tidal swimming pool, surfing, car park, café.

Widemouth Bay   An extensive sandy beach with flat reefs and rockpools: surfing, car park, café.

Falmouth area

Gyllyngvase   Wide sandy popular beach in town: café, car park.

Maenporth   Sheltered sandy family beach on an estuary: rock pools, café, car park.

Swanpool   Another sheltered sandy family beach with a café and car park.

Fowey area

Lansallos, nr Polperro   A small sheltered beach with steep access: walk from car park, no facilities.

Lantic Bay   Glorious sandy beach but with a long walk down steep cliff path (slippery after rain): NT car park, no facilities.

Turquoise seas at Porthcurno.

Cawsand Beach.

Polkerris Popular sheltered sandy beach enclosed by a stone harbor: café, uphill walk to car park.

Polridmouth Very quiet cove: walk from car park, no facilities.

Hayle/St Ives area
Gwithian The eastern end of a 3-mile (4¾km) long sandy dune-backed beach on St Ives Bay: surfing, cafés, car park.

Porthgwidden, St Ives Small sheltered sandy beach on the Island (St Ives' Head): café, car park.

Porthmeor, St Ives A long sandy beach by Tate St Ives: gently shelving, surfing, café, car park.

Porthminster, St Ives This is a large, sandy, gently shelving beach: surfing, café, car park.

Isles of Scilly area (p 164)
Bryher Great Par, Rushy Bay, Green Bay.

St Agnes Periglis, Cove Vean.

St Martin's Great Bay, Par Beach by Higher Town Quay and Middle Town Beach.

St Mary's Town Beach, Porthcressa, Porth Mellon, Old Town Bay, Porth Hellick.

Tresco Green Porth, New Grimsby, Pentle Bay, Appletree Bay.

Lands End area
Nanjizal (Mill Bay) Beautiful sandy beach with rock pools: only accessible by foot, no facilities.

Porthcurno Popular, white-sand beach with turquoise sea: café, car park.

Whitesand Bay, Sennen Cove A huge sandy beach: gently shelving, surfing, café, car park.

Lizard area
Church Cove, Helston A pretty sandy cove with a stream; features a 15th-century church and marshes behind, plus rock pools, café and a car park.

Coverack Sheltered shingly beach, popular with families: cafés, car park.

Kennack Sands A sandy family beach (and nature reserve with fascinating geology): rock pools, surfers, kiosk, car park.

Kynance Cove Picture-postcard beach in rugged NT setting: cliffs, white sands, café, walk from car park (seasonal toll); beware tidal cutoff points and loose rocks.

Poldhu Cove, Mullion Sandy beach: rock pools, car park, no facilities.

Looe area
Cawsand A sand/shingle beach: rock pools, café, car park.

Downderry A wide sand/shingle beach: café, car park.

Portwrinkle Quiet sand/shingle beach: rock pools, steep access, car park, no facilities.

Seaton Popular grey sandy family beach: café, car park.

Talland Bay A lovely shingle/sand family beach: rock pools, cafés, car park.

Town Beach, Looe Small popular sandy family beach: café, car park.

Whitsand Bay A 3-mile (4¾km) long sandy beach: surfing, steep access, car parks, no facilities.

Newquay area
Crantock Beach A pleasant sandy beach with extensive dunes: car park, no facilities.

Fistral Beach, Newquay
The UK's top surfing beach: a huge expanse of bright sand with pounding breakers, café and car park.

Holywell Bay A broad sandy beach with sand dunes: surfing, café, car park.

Mawgan Porth Wide sandy beach backed by cliffs and dunes: surfing, café, car park (good views).

Porth, Newquay Deep stream-cove backed by low cliffs (busy road behind): sandy, café, car park.

Porth Joke (Jolly) Narrow sandy cove with caves and rock pools: surfing, car park, no facilities.

Watergate Bay, Newquay
A 2-mile (3¼km) long sandy beach: popular, surfing, café, car park, Jamie Oliver's Fifteen (p 123).

Padstow area
Boobys Bay Wide sandy beach with dunes, rock pools, surfing; A walk from Constantine car park, no facilities.

Constantine Bay Long sandy beach with dunes behind and seaward reefs: surfing, small car park, no facilities.

Daymer Bay, Rock Large, popular family beach in a lovely setting: sandy, rock pools, sheltered, café, car park (superb views).

Harlyn Bay Popular family beach with a stream and rocky headlands: sandy, rock pools, surfing, café, car park.

Porthcothan Pleasant family stream-cove of sand and shingle, backed by dunes: shop, car park.

St George's Cove, Harbour Cove, Hawker's Cove Long, sandy beaches on an estuary (huge at low tide): only accessible on foot, rural setting, no facilities.

Whitesand Bay, Sennen Cove.

Yellow flags at Porth Joke.

Treyarnon Bay Popular family beach: sandy, rock pools, surfing, café, car park.

Penzance area
Mount's Bay, Penzance A vast sandy/pebbly beach with a café and car park (and views of St Michael's Mount).

Perranuthnoe Sandy, rocky, popular family beach: café, car park.

Praa Sands A 1½-mile (2½km) long, popular, sandy beach (with steep access): surfing, café, car park.

Perranporth/St Agnes area
Chapel Porth Small sandy cove backed by grassy cliffs (unstable): wide beach at low tide, surfing, kiosk, car park.

Perranporth A 2-mile (3¼km) long sandy beach divided by headland at high water: sand dunes, surfing, café, car park (good views).

Porthtowan Spacious sandy beach with unstable cliffs behind: rock pools, seawater pool, surfing, café, car park.

Trevaunance Cove Narrow shingle and sandy cove with unusual rocks and caves: surfing, café, car park.

Polzeath area
Polzeath A very popular estuarial beach of fine, gleaming sand, rock pools: surfing, café, car park; quieter Pentireglaze Haven is at New Polzeath.

Trebarwith Strand Long sandy beach in a pretty setting (access via narrow lanes) that disappears at high tide. Access is over dark 'filo pastry' rocks: surfing, car park, café; freak waves and rockfall hazards.

Roseland Peninsula area
Gorran Haven A small sandy village beach: shop, car park.

Trebarwith Strand at the height of summer.

Surfing

Over the last 20 years surfing and its associated paraphernalia—surfboard and wetsuit hire, beach bars and cafés, sport clothing shops—have boomed; an estimated 250,000 people surf in the UK today, and the vast majority do it on the coasts of Devon and Cornwall. Newquay in particular is considered one of the world's premier surfing resorts.

If you want to have a go, contact the local Tourist Information Centre (TIC) or ask someone at the beach; many surf schools have mobile information points. There is usually a minimum age limit for lessons (around 8 years old); prices typically start at around £25 for 2 hours. On the main beaches surfing and bathing zones are segregated by chequered flags.

Here are some of Cornwall's surfing hotspots, suitable for all abilities:

North coast (running east–west):
Crooklets Beach and Summerleaze Beach, Bude;
Polzeath and Harlyn Bay near Padstow;
Watergate Bay and Fistral Beach—the best and most famous—in Newquay; nearby Holywell Bay;
Perranporth;
Gwithian Towans;
Whitesand Bay at Sennen Cove near Lands End.

South coast (running west–east):
Praa Sands;
Pentewan Beach;
Whitsand Bay on the Rame Peninsula.

Visit www.bbc.co.uk/cornwall/surfing/surfingguide.shtml for more details.

Little and Great Molunan
Two small, sheltered, sandy family beaches: rock pools, walk from car park, no facilities.

Par Sands   Wide sandy popular family beach: café, car park.

Pendower/Carne   A 1-mile (1½km) long sandy beach in rural setting: dunes, café, car park.

Pentewan   Large busy sandy beach: café, car park.

Porthbeor   A lovely remote sandy beach with rock pools: walk from car park, no facilities.

Porthcurnick, Portscatho   A wide sandy beach: rock pools, café, parking (views).

Porthluney Cove, Caerhayes
Quiet sandy family beach backed by wooded cliffs: rock pools, kiosk, car park.

Porthpean, St Austell   A small sheltered family beach: rock pools, shop, car park.

Towan   Long sandy beach with low sand dunes and rock pools: car park, no facilities.

Active Cornwall

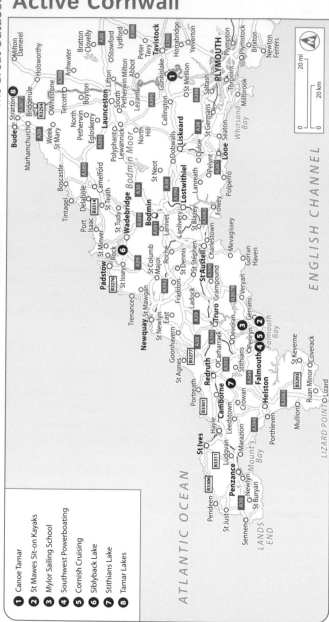

1. Canoe Tamar
2. St Mawes Sit-on Kayaks
3. Mylor Sailing School
4. Southwest Powerboating
5. Cornish Cruising
6. Siblyback Lake
7. Stithians Lake
8. Tamar Lakes

ATLANTIC OCEAN

ENGLISH CHANNEL

Falmouth Bay

Whitsand Bay

Mount's Bay

LANDS END

LIZARD POINT

Cornwall offers a vast range of outdoor activities: from walking a section of the South West Coast Path or cycling along a disused railway line to kite surfing and sand yachting (p 90), plus climbing (p 73), horse-riding (p 90) or enjoying a round of golf on one of the county's many fine courses (p 89). Add to that the attractions of the sea and inland waters—swimming and surfing (p 71), sailing and windsurfing, seafishing (p 90), canoeing and kayaking—and it's clear that all tastes and abilities are catered for. Contact the local TIC for detailed information.

Getting Active on Foot

Few would argue that Cornwall's coastline is the jewel in the county's crown. The incomparable scenery, constantly shifting light and mild weather provide plenty of encouragement to get out in the fresh air. The South West Coast Path (Britain's longest National Trail at 630 miles (1014km) from Minehead in Somerset to Poole in Dorset) provides opportunities for all levels of stamina, from a gentle stroll along a beach to a tough trek up and down the steep-sided combes (valleys) of the north coast. You can try a simple there-and-back walk or work out a circular route from the relevant map; local TICs will be able to provide details of local walking guides. The Virtual Book Company publishes

The South West Coast Path north of Bude.

a DVD outlining more than 40 interactive walks along the South West Coast Path (www.virtualbook company.co uk). For more details about walking, contact the South West Coast Path Association (☎ 01752 896237; www.swcp.org. uk) and www.walkcornwall.com.

Safety First

The walks described on pp 76–83 are all suitable for anyone relatively fit, but the South West Coast Path can be a strenuous experience. The terrain is variable and may involve clambering over boulders or negotiating rough steps. Make sure that you have adequate footwear (boots or strong walking shoes), take water and a bite to eat, and be prepared for changeable weather (take a layer or two of warm, waterproof clothing). Don't use the South West Coast Path in high winds (especially on the north coast), avoid unstable cliff edges and keep dogs under control at all times (on leads when passing through farmland). If you're doing anything other than a simple there-and-back route, take the relevant Ordnance Survey map and know how to use it.

Kayaking on the Bude Canal

The **Saints' Way** (Forth an Syns), a route first established in 1984, runs for 30 miles (48km) across Cornwall, linking the churches of St Petroc in Padstow (p 94) and St Fimbarrus in Fowey (p 105). A similar overland route known as the Mariners' Way was once used by traders who wished to avoid the dangerous sea journey around Land's End.

The **Copper Trail,** a circular route around Bodmin Moor, devised in 2005, has greatly improved the scope for waymarked walking in this area.

On the Cornish Way near Penzance.

Roughly 60 miles (96km) in length, the trail splits easily into six sections of 6–13 miles (9½–21km), and includes historic sites such as Minions and St Neot (p 19 and p 143), as well as the main towns and villages such as Bodmin and St Breward (p 93 and p 145). For more information on walking on Bodmin Moor, visit www.bobm.info/short-walks.htm.

Getting Active on Wheels

Cycling is prohibited on the South West Coast Path, and Cornwall's narrow, high-hedged lanes are not ideal for cycling, but a number of disused railways and tramways now provide excellent safe cycle routes. The **Camel Trail** (p 85) is one of the best known and most popular. The **Mineral Tramways Coast-to-Coast** from Portreath Harbour (near Redruth) to Devoran (on the Carrick Roads) is slightly more ambitious, but is an ideal way of getting into the heart of the Gwennap Mining District (part of the World Heritage Site, p 81). An easy off-road trail runs from Pentewan on the south coast to St Austell (with road links to the Eden Project, p 40). The Eden Project also plays a leading role in a low-carbon

initiative called the **Clay Trails** (www.sustrans.org.uk); visitors arriving by bike or on foot pay a reduced entrance fee.

For more ambitious cyclists the **Cornish Way** (devised in 2002, linking National Cycle Routes 2, 3 and 32) combines several trails for cyclists and walkers, covering 180 miles (290km) from Bude near the Devon border all the way to Lands End (www.sustrans.org.uk). East of Bude the route continues through Devon and Somerset to Bristol.

Cycle lockers are available at major rail stations (Truro, St Austell, Liskeard and Penzance) for a small fee; TICs can provide information about cycle hire. See also www.visitcornwall.com and www.cyclecornwall.com.

Getting Active on Water

The extensive estuaries of the Cornish coast are extremely popular for sailing. Thousands of pleasure craft are moored here all year round, and the number of visiting vessels rockets in summer: around 7,000 yachts visit Fowey annually. Some of the best estuarial sailing waters include the Lynher (which feeds into Plymouth Sound), the Fowey, the Carrick Roads, the Helford and the Camel.

If you want to learn or improve your skills, contact local TICs. You can paddle up the Tamar in a

Dinghies on Town Beach, East Looe

Canadian canoe from Morwellham Quay (**1 Canoe Tamar** ☎ 0845 4301208; www.canoetamar.co.uk), potter round quiet creeks near St Mawes on a kayak (**2 St Mawes Sit-on Kayaks** ☎ 07981 846786; www.stmaweskayaks.co.uk), learn to sail a dinghy or keelboat on the Fal (**3 Mylor Sailing School** ☎ 01326 377633; www.mylorsailingschool.co.uk), be taught how to cope with a powerboat (**4 Southwest Powerboating** ☎ 01326 211021; www.southwestpowerboating.co.uk), or charter a yacht and cruise to the Isles of Scilly (**5 Cornish Cruising** ☎ 01326 211800, for instance; www.cornishcruising.com). Make sure that whatever company you choose is RYA (Royal Yacht Association) approved.

Inland Waters

If the thought of taking to the open sea in a boat isn't for you, Cornwall's safe inland waters under the care of the South West Lakes Trust may be more to your liking. Three venues have watersports centres, offering sailing, windsurfing, canoeing, kayaking and rowing (as well as angling): **6 Siblyback Lake** on Bodmin Moor (☎ 01779 346522); **7 Stithians Lake** near Redruth (☎ 01209 860301); and **8 Tamar Lakes** near Bude (☎ 01288 321712). These all offer a range of courses and boat or equipment rental. For more details, visit www.swlakestrust.org.uk.

Walk One: **Round Stepper Point to Padstow (north coast)**

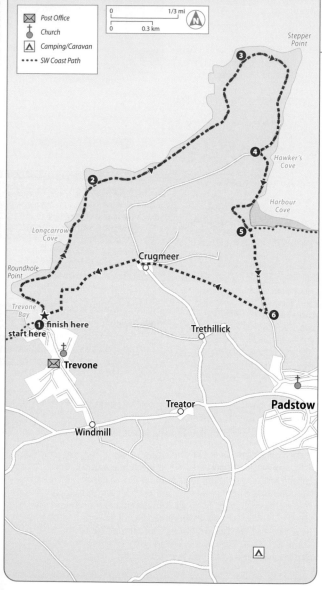

Unlike much of Cornwall's rugged north coast, the section round Stepper Point from Trevone to Padstow is fairly level and easy underfoot, apart from one short sharp climb at Gunver Head. This 6½-mile (10½km) 3-hour route is stunningly beautiful, running inland up the broad and tranquil Camel estuary to the bustling little town of Padstow, before a gentle return to Trevone through fields. Maps: OS Explorer 106, Landranger 200.

1 From **Trevone beach,** follow the South West Coast Path signs north-east towards low cliffs, and carry on past **Round Hole Point.** Take care—the Round Hole is a collapsed sea cave that forms a huge cavity in the cliff-top. Follow the South West Coast Path signs along Marble Cliff (unusually formed of limestone here, in contrast to the slate along most of the north Cornwall coast). The path undulates through two small combes, and then climbs very steeply up to **Gunver Head.** Notice the miniature 'islands' offshore, (detached sections of cliff). The path is near the cliff edge here so take care when it's windy.

2 Continue along the South West Coast Path to **Stepper Point,** composed of tough greenstone; look out for bands of green and purple slate in the cliff face at **Butter Hole.** Walk on past the **Pepperpot,** a daymark constructed in 1832 as a navigation aid for shipping.

3 Follow the South West Coast Path inland along the edge of the peaceful Camel estuary as far as **Hawker's Cove.** The large building dates from 1847; it sheltered pilots who helped vessels negotiate the Doom Bar, a shifting estuarial sandbank on which over 300 vessels foundered between 1760 and 1920. The old lifeboat station here was abandoned in 1967 when the Padstow lifeboat moved to a more accessible spot on Mother Ivey's Bay to the south.

4 Continue up the estuary; across the water you can see Brae Hill and the little church of St Enodoc nestling in the sand dunes, where the former poet laureate Sir John Betjeman was buried in 1984. At **Sandy Harbour Cove,** follow the South West Coast Path signs inland and across a footbridge, and then along a field edge to meet a track; turn right.

5 Where the South West Coast Path is signed to the left, carry straight on as far as **Tregirls Farm.** Walk down the drive and along the lane.

6 Just over the brow of the hill (for **Prideaux Place** (p 59) and **Padstow** keep straight on, adding 1 mile [1½km] there and back) turn right over a stile. Follow the signed path through fields to **Crugmeer;** turn left on the lane and then right at the junction and immediately left on another lane, which leads back to the beach at **Trevone.**

The South West Coast Path towards Stepper Point.

Walk Two: **Porthcurno & Logan Rock (south coast)**

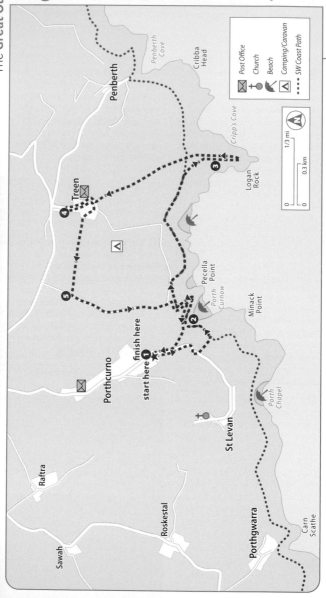

Post Office
Church
Beach
Camping/Caravan
SW Coast Path

Penberth Cove
Cribba Head
Cripp's Cove
Penberth
Treen
Logan Rock
Pecella Point
Porth Curnow
Minack Point
finish here
start here
Porthcurno
St Levan
Porth Chapel
Raftra
Roskestal
Sawah
Porthgwarra
Carn Scathe

The turquoise waters and white sandy beach at Porthcurno attract hundreds of holidaymakers in the summer season, but the South West Coast Path near this lovely cove deserves exploration too. This 3½-mile (5½km) walk takes in the Minack Theatre (p 35), an international telegraph station, an Iron Age fortification, a logan (rocking) stone, a pub and two cafés in just under 2 hours. Maps: OS Explorer 102, Landranger 203.

1 Start from the beach car park and turn left up the lane (steep). At the hilltop turn left to find the **Minack Theatre.** Follow the South West Coast Path signs to the left of the entrance and climb down boulder steps, and then follow the path inland to meet a path junction at the back of the beach.

2 Follow the South West Coast Path up the other side of the beach, passing a **pillbox.** At the next junction turn right, and soon right again to find a **white pyramid** marking the spot where the submarine telegraph cable from Brest ran ashore in 1880: (Porthcurno Telegraph Museum, p 35). Rejoin the South West Coast Path, and soon turn right on a narrow path along the cliff edge past **Treen Cove** before rejoining the main South West Coast Path again. Views of the **Logan Rock** are particularly good from here. Turn right on the South West Coast Path to reach an old NT contributions cairn.

3 Bear right and walk out towards **Logan Rock,** passing through the Iron Age earthworks of **Treryn**

The Logan Rock at Porthcurno.

Dinas (castle). Retrace your steps to the cairn and keep ahead, following the signed path through fields to reach the lane in **Treen.** Turn right for the café, and then left downhill to find the **Logan Rock pub.**

4 Retrace your steps uphill from the pub; where the lane bears left, keep ahead and then right, as signed. Follow the signed path through the fields to reach **Trendrennan Farm.**

5 Turn left and pass through a blue-waymarked gate to the left of a stile. This path leads gently downhill to rejoin the South West Coast Path. Turn right, and stay on that path to meet a track. Turn right for the beach car park.

The Logan Rock

Logan stones occur in areas of granite, which weathers and cracks in distinctive ways. In 1824, the famous Logan Rock at Porthcurno was permanently dislodged by a high-spirited group of naval recruits led by Lieutenant Goldsmith. He was ordered by the Admiralty to replace the stone at his own expense.

The Great Outdoors

Walk Three: **St Agnes Beacon (north coast)**

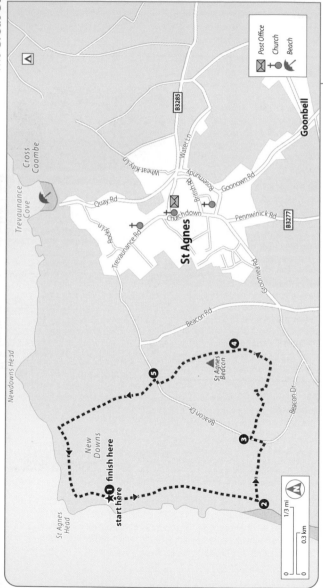

Cornwall's industrial past is proudly stamped on the north coast near St Agnes, part of the Cornish Mining World Heritage Site (below). Towanroath engine house, built in 1872, is perched on the steep cliff edge, stealing the show on many a postcard and calendar. This 3½-mile (5½km) walk passes through the tin-mining area, and climbs to the top of St Agnes Beacon, where the legendary Giant Bolster was big enough to stand with one foot on the beacon and the other on Carn Brea above Redruth, several miles inland. Maps: OS Explorer 104, Landranger 203.

1 From the parking area on the coast at **Carn Gowla** follow the South West Coast Path past dressed granite blocks towards the restored mine buildings at **Wheal Coates.** Walk on past **Stamps and Whim** engine houses; look back down for a good view of **Towanroath.** Retrace your steps to Stamps and Whim.

2 Turn right inland on a path, soon passing a chimney, and eventually meeting a lane by a car park. Turn left.

3 Turn right up the drive to **Beacon Farm,** continuing through the farmyard to find three gates. Go through the left gate as signed on the footpath and walk around the left edge of the field and over a stile on to the beacon. Follow the narrow path to the left before climbing to the trig point at 620ft (189m). On a clear day, views stretch for 30 miles (48km).

4 From the trig point, walk along the ridge ahead, taking the right of two obvious paths. This path

The stile leads onto St Agnes Beacon.

eventually bears left round the hill, back towards the coast. When you can see the lane below you on the right, turn right downhill on a narrow path to meet it, and turn right.

5 Almost immediately turn left down a signed track. Follow this in a straight line across a bank and track; keep ahead to meet the South West Coast Path. Turn left to return to your car.

Mining World Heritage Site

In 2006, the Cornwall and West Devon Mining World Heritage Site was established by UNESCO, in recognition of the contribution made by the area to Britain's industrial revolution and its influence on mining worldwide. Five of these lie on the South West Coast Path: St Just, Hayle, Portreath Harbour, Wheal Coates (see **1** above) and Wheal Trewavas near Praa Sands. For more information, visit www.cornish-mining.org.uk.

Walk Four: **St Anthony Head (south coast)**

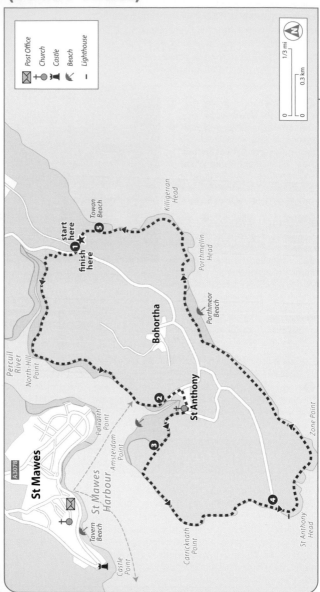

The Carrick Roads, a huge multi-pronged estuary between Falmouth and St Mawes, has been protected against foreign invaders since Tudor times (see Pendennis Castle, p 58). To the east stands the 19th-century lighthouse on St Anthony Head, site of a beacon in earlier times, which was lit to warn mariners of the dangers of the Manacles reef offshore. Various fortifications survive here from World War II. This 6-mile (10km) walk, though lengthy, isn't too strenuous. The views en route are stunning, and there's the chance to visit several lovely beaches. Maps: OS Explorer 105, Landranger 204.

❶ From the car park at **Porth Farm,** follow the footpath sign for **Percuil river** and **Place Quay.** The path runs beside **Porth Creek** and then into woodland. Follow the narrow, root-strewn path as it bears left along the Percuil river, soon passing **St Mawes** on the opposite bank (p 59). After the ferry (to St Mawes) point at **Torr's Steps,** walk through meadows to reach **Place Quay. Place House** (dating from 1840 on an earlier site) stands opposite where you emerge onto the lane.

❷ Turn left up the lane, and then right over a stile (signed St Anthony Head) to pass through the atmospheric graveyard and 12th-century church of **St Anthony-in-Roseland** (note the superb Norman south door). Follow the signed path past the church, soon turning right on a track to reach **Cellars Beach;** the cottages here were once used to store pilchards.

❸ Turn left where signed over a stile and keep uphill beside a field; at the top, cross another stile and drop down to the coast. Turn left along low cliffs and follow the coast path all the way to the car park at **St Anthony Battery,** passing lovely **Great Molunan** beach on the way.

❹ Turn right and take the tarmac path round the end of the point past gun emplacements and an observation post. Rejoin the coast path and keep ahead, eventually passing **Porthbeor beach.** Keep on round **Porthmellin** and **Killigerran Heads** to reach **Towan beach** (*towan* is Cornish for sand dune).

❺ Turn left at the beach up an old sanding road, once used to transport seaweed (used as an agricultural fertiliser) by donkey from the beach. Cross the lane back to the car park at **Porth Farm.**

View to Falmouth from St Anthony Head.

Cycle One: **The Camel Trail**

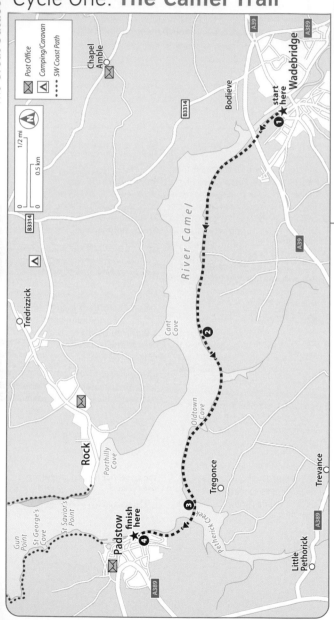

The Camel Trail is an off-road cycling and walking route along the line of the former Bodmin & Wadebridge railway. The railway was originally used to export slate, granite, tin, iron and copper from Bodmin Moor, and to carry lime-rich marine sand inland to be used as fertiliser. The branch line linking it to Padstow opened in 1889. In terms of visitor numbers, the Camel Trail ranks third among Cornwall's attractions, with around 350,000 users each year. It's ideal for families: a safe, level route along one of Cornwall's most beautiful estuaries, which can be picked up at various points along its 18-mile (29km) length. The trail starts at Poley's Bridge near Blisland on Bodmin Moor, and runs via Bodmin and Wadebridge before the scenic waterfront stretch to Padstow. In the height of the holiday season it's far less stressful to use this route than trying to drive into Padstow. **START: Wadebridge, using the car park on Eddystone Road. Trip length: 10 miles (16km). Time: 1 hr minimum (excluding picnic time); alternatively, you can simply cycle 26 miles (42km) there and back inland to Poley's Bridge. For more information visit www.ncdc.gov.uk or www.sustrans.org.uk.**

Join the trail at **Wadebridge**. From here you can choose the quieter option of cycling inland through a wooded valley to Bodmin (p 93) or take the more popular route along the Camel estuary to **Padstow** (described below).

1 Follow the track leading under the A39 road bridge, with the **Camel river** to your right. Granite used to rebuild the Eddystone lighthouse, which stands 14 miles (22½km) off the coast at Plymouth in Devon, was shipped out from Wadebridge Quay in the 19th century.

2 A long cutting ends at the spoil heaps of old slate quarries. The Camel estuary and its sandbanks provide a home for thousands of migrant wildfowl in winter, as well as indigenous species such as oystercatcher and curlew. Continue on past **Pinkson Creek**.

3 Cross the bridge over **Little Petherick Creek**. The **Saints' Way** (p 74) follows the creek at this point. Ahead of you, notice the obelisk on **Dennis Hill**, which commemorates Queen Victoria's silver jubilee in 1887.

4 Follow the trail into **Padstow**, arriving via the quayside car park (p 125).

Cycle Hire
Bike Smart (Wadebridge) ☎ 01208 814545.

Bridge Bike Hire (Wadebridge) ☎ 01208 813050; www.bridgebike hire.co.uk.

Camel Trail Cycle Hire (Wadebridge) ☎ 01208 814104.

Padstow Cycle Hire (Padstow) ☎ 01841 533533; www.padstow cyclehire.com.

Trail Bike Hire (Padstow) ☎ 01841 532594; www.trailbikehire.co.uk.

The Camel Trail between Wadebridge and Padstow.

Cycle Two: **The Coast-to-Coast Trail**

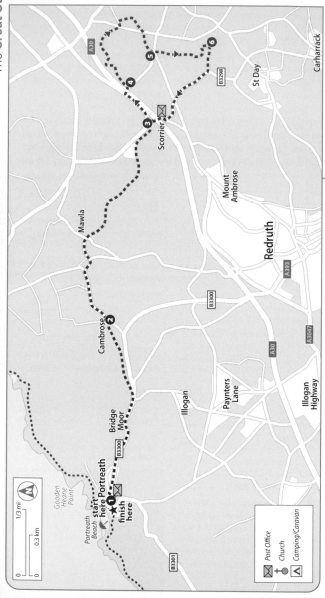

The Coast-to-Coast Trail runs for 11 miles (17½km) across Cornwall, following the line of two early horse-drawn tramways, the Portreath Tramroad (started in 1809) and the Redruth & Chasewater Railway (opened in 1830 and then steam-driven from the mid-19th century). The trail links the old mining harbours of Portreath (near Redruth) on the north coast with Devoran (north of Falmouth) on the south. The section from Scorrier in mid-Cornwall to Portreath operated from 1812 until the mid-1860s, and by 1827 Portreath was one of Cornwall's busiest ports. The cycle ride described below runs from Portreath to Scorrier, and then follows the Wheal Busy Loop, a slightly tougher section that explores an area of disused mine-workings before returning along the tramroad to Portreath. START: Portreath. Trip length: 13½ miles (21¾km). Time: 3 hr (excluding picnic time); alternatively, you can simply cycle the 11 miles (19¼km) to Devoran and back along the Coast-to-Coast Trail. Park in Portreath car park. www. visitcornwall.com.

❶ From the car park turn left on the B3300 and cycle inland. Turn left along **Sunny Vale Road**; where this bears right, fork left on to the tramway (waymarked throughout by an engine house on a lump of granite block). Follow the track to reach the road at **Cambrose**.

❷ Turn left to pass **Elm Farm** (cycle hire—see below). After about 500 yards (½km) turn right to a T-junction at **Lower Forge**; cross over, and keep ahead at the next T-junction back onto the tramway. Follow this to **North Downs**; turn left, and then right on the pavement to the roundabout.

❸ Turn left across the road, with the roundabout to your right. Keep uphill over another small roundabout; turn right over the A30 at the hilltop.

❹ Just over the bridge turn left on a rough track; follow the track past the old **Boscawen Mine**. Pass **Wheal Busy chapel** to a lane junction and keep ahead, after around 100 yards (100m) turn right on a bridlepath, and then right on a track. Head to the left of **old mine buildings at Wheal Busy,** and keep

ahead uphill, crossing a lane and bearing left to a road.

❺ Cross over and head downhill past **Hawke's Shaft pumping house** (which has Cornwall's tallest chimney stack) into **Unity Woods**, keeping left at the fork to meet a junction.

❻ Turn right, rejoining the tramway. Leave the woods and cross the B3298 as signed and follow the track along the left side of the road. Turn left along the pavement, and then right across the road to pass the pub. At the next road turn left under the railway bridge; at the T-junction cross over and then turn right to cross the A30 and rejoin the outward route.

Cycle Hire
Bissoe Tramways Cycle Hire
☎ 01872 870341; www.cornwall cyclehire.com.

Elm Farm, Cambrose, Portreath
☎ 01208 891498; www.elm-farm. co.uk.

Higher Laity Farm, Portreath
☎ 01209 842317; www.higherlaity farm.co.uk.

The Best **of the Rest**

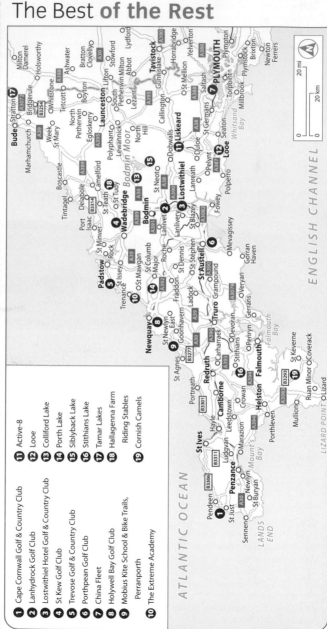

1 Cape Cornwall Golf & Country Club
2 Lanhydrock Golf Club
3 Lostwithiel Hotel Golf & Country Club
4 St Kew Golf Club
5 Trevose Golf & Country Club
6 Porthpean Golf Club
7 China Fleet
8 Holywell Bay Golf Club
9 Mobius Kite School & Bike Trails, Perranporth
10 The Extreme Academy

11 Active-8
12 Looe
13 Colliford Lake
14 Porth Lake
15 Siblyback Lake
16 Stithians Lake
17 Tamar Lakes
18 Hallagenna Farm Riding Stables
19 Cornish Camels

Golf

Cornwall has some of the most scenic golf courses in the UK, many in spectacular coastal settings, some with top-class clubhouse and hotel and/or self-catering facilities. **❶ Cape Cornwall Golf & Country Club** near St Just (☎ 01736 788611; www.capecornwall.com) is Britain's 'first and last' 18-hole course (that is, the farthest west) with amazing views. Courses are fairly evenly distributed throughout the county; a selection is listed below.

Inland Courses

❷ Lanhydrock Golf Club (p 95) promises rural tranquillity at a charming18-hole parkland course (☎ 01208 262570; www.lanhydrockhotel.com).

❸ Lostwithiel Hotel Golf & Country Club is an 18-hole course in the beautiful wooded valley of the River Fowey (☎ 01208 873350).

❹ St Kew Golf Club, a 9-hole course near Wadebridge, offers special Saturday rates for families (☎ 01208 841500).

Coastal Courses

❺ Trevose Golf & Country Club at Constantine Bay near Padstow is a Championship course making the most of a stunning stretch of the north coast. Enjoy the views, and try not to be daunted by the blustery winds (☎ 01841 520208; www.trevose-gc.co.uk).

❻ Porthpean Golf Club is a challenging 18-hole course with a driving range overlooking St Austell Bay on the south coast (☎ 01726 64613; www.porthpeangolfclub.co.uk).

❼ China Fleet is set in 180 acres (73 hectares) bordering the River Tamar in southeast Cornwall near Saltash (☎ 01752 848465; www.china-fleet.co.uk).

❽ Holywell Bay Golf Club near Newquay adopts an informal approach to the sport (☎ 01637 832916; www.holywellbay.co.uk): no membership; no handicap; no dress code; and no booking required.

See www.visitcornwall.co.uk for more details, and get hold of a copy

Golf course with view of the Newquay coast.

of the Cornwall Golf Map, published annually by Indigo Publishing (☎ 01566 785628; www.indigo-publishing.co.uk), and available in most TICs.

Extreme Sports

In recent years there has been a huge increase in the number of people choosing to have a go at adventure sports such as coasteering (traversing the cliffs between land and sea), kitesurfing (a cross between windsurfing and power kiting), mountain boarding (skateboarding on rough terrain) and sand yachting (exactly how it sounds!), and the sea cliffs around Bosigran in West Penwith are a great draw for rock-climbers. Specialist companies have sprung up to meet the demand. Three examples based in Cornwall include:

❾ Mobius Kite School & Bike Trails (☎ 08456 430630; www.mobiusonline.co.uk) in Perranporth Hayle, Marazion and Pentewan.

❿ The Extreme Academy at Watergate Bay (☎ 01637 860543; www.watergatebay.co.uk).

⓫ Active-8 near Liskeard (☎ 01579 320848; www.active cornwall.co.uk).

A couple of horse riders on Gwithian beach.

Fishing

The fishing industry has played a vital role in Cornwall's economy for hundreds of years. Although commercial fishing has declined, leisure- and sport-fishing have become very big business; every port and village along the coast offers sea-fishing trips of some kind. Just take a walk along the quay and see what's on offer.
⓬ Looe (p 113) is the acknowledged shark-fishing centre of Great Britain, although some are uncomfortable with the ethics of this pursuit (Shark Angling Club of GB ☎ 01503 262642). Fishing for stillwater trout is available at **⓭ Colliford Lake** near Bodmin (☎ 01579 346522) and **⓮ Porth Lake** near Newquay (☎ 01566 771930; www.swlakes trust.org.uk), plus **⓯ Siblyback, ⓰ Stithians** and the **⓱ Tamar Lakes,** p 75). See www.visit cornwall.com and click on the external link for a fuller list of Cornwall's inland fishing waters.

Horse Riding

One of the most satisfying and relaxing ways of exploring the Cornish countryside is on horseback.

⓲ Hallagenna Farm Riding Stables at St Breward on Bodmin Moor (☎ 01208 851500; www.hallagenna.co.uk) offers pony trekking and trail rides for all levels of experience, including a pub ride to The Blisland Inn (p 95). See www.visitcornwall.com and click on the external link for a list of Cornish riding schools. For something completely different, head for the Lizard Peninsula and have a go at camel trekking with **⓳ Cornish Camels** (☎ 01326 231119; www.cornish camels.com). ●

Bodmin

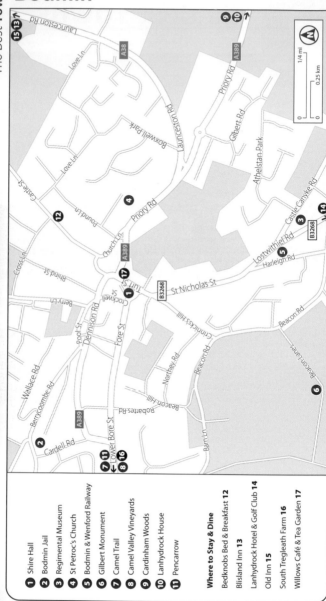

1 Shire Hall
2 Bodmin Jail
3 Regimental Museum
4 St Petroc's Church
5 Bodmin & Wenford Railway
6 Gilbert Monument
7 Camel Trail
8 Camel Valley Vineyards
9 Cardinham Woods
10 Lanhydrock House
11 Pencarrow

Where to Stay & Dine

Bedknobs Bed & Breakfast 12
Blisland Inn 13
Lanhydrock Hotel & Golf Club 14
Old Inn 15
South Tregleath Farm 16
Willows Café & Tea Garden 17

Previous page: View of Fowey from Polruan.

Cornwall's former county town lies on the western edge of the lonely moor to which it gives its name. Although not instantly seductive, this down-to-earth town has a fascinating military history and makes a convenient central base for exploring east Cornwall. The county court was held in Bodmin until 1988, when it moved to Truro, but the old court room along with its holding cells is now a compelling visitor attraction.

Bodmin's well-stocked **Tourist Information Centre** (☎ 01208 76616; www.bodminmoor.co.uk or www.bodminlive.com), **Bodmin Town Museum** (☎ 01208 77607, Easter–Sept Mon–Fri 10:30am–6pm, Sat 10:30am–2:30pm, closed Sun. Oct Mon–Fri 10:30am–2:30pm. Closed Sun and Bank Holidays) and **Bodmin Court Room Experience** (☎ 01208 76616/79898; adult £3.25, child £2.25, family £10, concessions £2.75; court sessions hourly spring/summer Mon–Sat 11am–4pm, winter Mon–Fri 11am–4pm) share premises in the historic **❶ Shire Hall,** a monumental building in the heart of town. The Court Room Experience re-enacts the notorious real-life trial in 1844 of Matthew Weeks, accused of murdering Charlotte Dymond on Rough Tor; the audience can vote 'guilty' or 'not guilty'. ⏲ *1½ hr Shire Hall, Mount Folly PL31 2DQ.*

❷ Bodmin Jail. Cornwall's infamous county jail, which closed in 1927, is now an all-weather family attraction, making much of executions and haunting: easy access to the Camel Trail. ⏲ *2 hr. Berrycombe Road PL31 2NR.* ☎ *01208 76292. www.bodminjail.org. Adult £5.50, child (ages 5–16) £3.25, concessions £3.75. Jail open all year 10am–dusk; bike hire 8am–dusk. Restaurant.*

❸ Regimental Museum. Dedicated to the Duke of Cornwall's Light Infantry, this museum occupies the old quartermaster's stores. The regiment's finest hour was the defence of Lucknow in 1857. The regimental Colours from 1816 hang in St Petroc's Church. ⏲ *1½ hr. The Keep, Lostwithiel Road PL31 1EG.*

Shire Hall.

Bodmin Moor

Once off the A30, you enter a world of narrow lanes, solid stone farms, archaeological remains and mining sites (p 19). Part of the same granite batholith (a large mass of igneous rock that has melted and intruded surrounding strata at great depths) that forms Dartmoor, West Penwith and the Isles of Scilly, Bodmin Moor is a designated AONB (Area of Outstanding Natural Beauty). Its highest point is Brown Willy at 1375ft (419m), source of the River Fowey (an old name for the area was 'Foweymoor'). Evidence of occupation dates back to the Bronze Age. China clay was extracted here from 1862 until 2001, and Bodmin granite was used to build the British Museum and Westminster Bridge.

☎ *01208 72810. www.lightinfantry. org.uk. Free admission. Mon–Fri, 9am–5pm.*

❹ St Petroc's Church. Cornwall's largest parish church dates mostly from the mid-15th century, but part of the tower and a superb carved font are Norman. St Petroc, founder of Bodmin, arrived from Ireland in about A.D. 600. The town remained the religious capital of Cornwall until the end of the Middle Ages. ⏱ *30 min. www.st-petroc-bodmin.co.uk.*

❺ Bodmin & Wenford Railway. Steam train fans can still enjoy a ride along a stretch of this historic standard-gauge line between Bodmin Parkway (access to Lanhydrock, p 60) and Boscarne Junction (linking with the Camel Trail, p 85; bikes free). The railway first opened in 1834 and closed in 1967. ⏱ *1½ hr. General Station, PL31 1AQ. ☎ 0845 1259678. www. bodminandwenfordrailway.co.uk. Call for timetable/fares. Shop, refreshments.*

❻ Gilbert Monument. The 144ft (44m) granite obelisk stands on a hilltop above the town. It was erected in memory of General Sir

Walter Raleigh Gilbert, born in Bodmin in 1785. A descendant of the famous Tudor explorers whose name he shares, he led a distinguished military career in Bengal. ⏱ *20 min.*

Places of Interest Nearby
❼ Camel Trail. *See p 85.*

❽ Camel Valley Vineyards. An award-winning attraction offering tours and tastings (£7.50). ⏱ *1½ hr. Nanstallon, Bodmin. ☎ 01208 77959. www.camelvalley.com. Free admission. Wine sales year round Mon–Fri 10am–5pm; Easter–end Sept Sat; Sun on Bank Hol weekends only.*

❾ Cardinham Woods. Over 618 acres (250 hectares) of mixed woodland, steep-sided valleys and narrow ravines, with waymarked trails for walking, cycling and horse riding; there is a café. ⏱ *45 min–2 hr (for walks). Signed off the A38 and the A30 2 miles (3¼km) east of Bodmin. ☎ 01208 72577. www.forestry. gov.uk. Café in Cadinham Woods: 10:30am-4pm daily.*

❿ Lanhydrock House. *See p 60.*

⓫ Pencarrow. *See p 60.*

Where to **Stay & Dine**

★★ **Bedknobs Bed & Breakfast**
Very comfortable B&B accommodation in an elegant, spacious, Victorian villa close to Bodmin town centre. There are extensive wooded gardens with a terrace. Breakfast includes locally produced sausages plus eggs from a neighbour's free-range hens. *Polgwyn, Castle Street PL31 2DX.* ☎ *01208 77553. www. bedknobs.co.uk. 3 rooms. WiFi. £75–90 per room per night. MC, V.*

★★★ **Blisland Inn** Award-winning real ale pub overlooking the green, with cosily cluttered beams and lots of room inside and out ('Not a restaurant that sells drinks, but a pub that sells food'). Local produce is cooked to order: farmhouse ham, egg and chips, leek and mushroom bake, sandwiches and homemade puddings. The Camel Trail (p 85) is under 1 mile (1½km) away. *Blisland, nr Bodmin PL30 4JK.* ☎ *01208 850739. Mains £6.95–12.95. MC, V. Mon–Sat 11:30am–11pm, Sun midday–10:30pm.*

★★ **Lanhydrock Hotel & Golf Club** This golfing hotel promises 'affordable luxury'. Though large and modern, it has the personal touch. In a spectacular setting just south of Bodmin, the 18-hole golf course is one of the finest in Cornwall. The Nineteen Bistro and Bar offers a wide-ranging menu. *Lostwithiel Road PL30 5AQ.* ☎ *01208 262570. www.lanhydrockhotel.com. 42 rooms with broadband. £89–139 per room per night. MC, V.*

★★★ **Old Inn** Parts of this ancient ale house date back 1,000 years. Said to be the highest pub in Cornwall, it has low beams, slate floors and a roaring log fire. Local produce features strongly: fish and vegetarian specials, crab and crayfish sandwiches, pan-fried fresh cod, homemade spinach, mushroom and stilton roulade. Moorland Grills are on the menu and there's a carvery on Sunday. *Churchtown, St Breward PL30 4PP.* ☎ *01208 850711. www.theoldinnandrestaurant.co.uk. £6.95–14.95. MC, V. Mon– Sat 11am–11pm, Sun midday–10:30pm.*

★★★ **South Tregleath Farm**
This working dairy farm overlooks the Camel Valley 2½ miles (4km) northeast of Bodmin. It offers luxurious B&B accommodation in a sophisticated Mediterranean style. Bedrooms are tastefully decorated; the guests' sitting room is upstairs in the architect-designed extension. Coarse fishing is available on site (free for longer-term guests). *Washaway, Bodmin PL30 3AA.* ☎ *01208 72692. www.south-tregleath.co.uk. 3 rooms. WiFi. £60–80 per room per night. No credit cards.*

★★ **Willows Café & Tea Garden**
Friendly, cheerful café in the town centre, with a garden and children's play area. Good value traditional homemade fare: breakfasts, chunky soups, Sunday roasts, sausage and mash, panini, and wonderful cakes. Daily specials board and Cornish fare on sale. *2 Turf Street PL31 1DU.* ☎ *01208 78477. Mains £4.95–5.95. No credit cards. Daily 9am–3ish all year round; call re evening opening.*

Bude

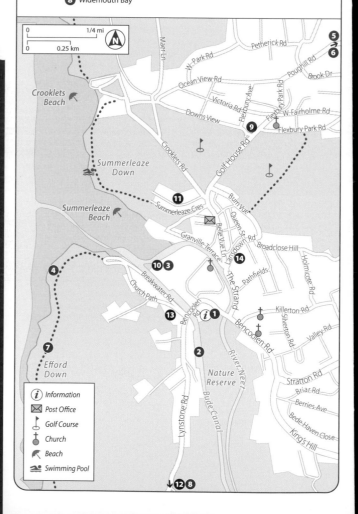

1 Bude Visitor Centre
2 Bude Canal
3 Castle Heritage Centre
4 Compass Point Storm Tower
5 Clovelly
6 Hartland Quay
7 South West Coast Path
8 Widemouth Bay

Where to Stay & Dine

Camelot Hotel **9**
Castle Restaurant **10**
Edgcumbe **11**
Elements **12**
The Falcon Hotel **13**
Ripe Café **14**

0   1/4 mi
0   0.25 km

Crooklets Beach

Summerleaze Down

Summerleaze Beach

Efford Down

i Information
✉ Post Office
⛳ Golf Course
✝ Church
☂ Beach
🏊 Swimming Pool

Petherick Rd
W. Park Rd
Ocean View Rd
Maer Ln
Poughill Rd
Brook Dr
Victoria Rd
Flexbury Ave
Downs View
W. Fairholme Rd
Flexbury Park Rd
Crooklets Rd
Golf House Rd
Summerleaze Cres
Burn Vue
Granville Terrace
Queen St
Bencoolen Rd
Bellevue Ln
Lansdown Rd
Broadclose Hill
Holmcote Rd
Breakwater Rd
Church Path
The Strand
Pathfields
Killerton Rd
Silverton Rd
Valley Rd
Bencoolen Rd
River Neet
Stratton Rd
Briar Rd
Berries Ave
Bede Haven Close
King's Hill
Nature Reserve
Bude Canal
Lynstone Rd

The little town of Bude resides on a low-lying stretch of the north coast a few miles south of the Devon border. In the Middle Ages there was just a chapel on a rock here, known as 'Bede's Haven'. From the 18th century until the early 20th, Bude was a thriving port, aided by the coming of the railway (and canal: see ❷ below). The demise of both in the 20th century forced Bude to turn to tourism as its main source of income. Today it's a popular beach and surfing resort, and provides a good base for exploring the north coast of Cornwall and Devon.

❶ **Bude Visitor Centre.** A helpful, well-stocked Tourist Information Centre (TIC), incorporating the Canal Visitor Centre (opened in 2007). ⏱ *30 min. Crescent Car Park EX23 8LE.* ☎ *01288 354240. www.visit bude.info.*

❷ **Bude Canal.** The canal opened in 1825, transporting coal, plus sand and limestone to use as a soil conditioner. The original ambitious plan to link this waterway with the Tamar at Calstock was never realised; at its longest the canal measured 35½ miles (57km). It fell into disrepair in the 1930s and only the Bude–Helebridge stretch remains navigable. It provides a haven for wildlife, and a walk along the towpath makes for a very pleasant afternoon; kayaks, rowing boats and bikes can be

Boats in the canal basin.

hired. The canal is currently undergoing extensive renovation. ⏱ *3 hr.*

❸ **Castle Heritage Centre.** Bude's 'castle' was built in 1830 (on sand, to prove it could be done!) by the eccentric inventor and scientist Sir Goldsworthy Gurney. Today it houses Bude's Heritage Centre (the Bude-Stratton Museum), with its gallery and restaurant. ⏱ *2 hr. The Wharf EX23 8LG.* ☎ *01288 357300. www.bude-stratton.org.uk. Adult £3.50, child (ages 5–15) £2.50, family £10, concessions £3. Daily 10am–4pm.*

❹ **Compass Point Storm Tower.** Also known as 'The Tower of the Winds', this eight-sided structure was built in the 1830s as a coastguard's shelter, its walls inscribed with the points of a compass. In the 1880s it was moved to its current position because of cliff erosion, and its orientation no longer matches the compass points. There are stunning views to the north over Bude's beaches. ⏱ *1 hr inc walk to get there.*

Places of Interest Nearby
❺ **Clovelly.** In Devon, 17 miles (27½km) north of Bude, is the little fishing village of Clovelly, one narrow and very steep cobbled street leading to a sheltered harbour. Donkeys used to haul sledges to transport goods up and down the street. Clovelly, owned by the same family since 1738, is extremely busy in season, and access is via the Visitor

Reverend Hawker

The little hamlet of Morwenstow is the last village near the coast before the Devon border on Cornwall's north coast. Its most famous resident was the eccentric Reverend Robert Stephen Hawker (1803–75), vicar of St Morwenna's church from 1831. He invented the harvest festival and wrote 'The Song of the Western Men', based on an old Cornish ballad, which includes the well-known lines 'And shall Trelawny die? Here's 20,000 Cornish men shall know the reason why.' He kept a close eye out for shipwrecks, insisting that every drowned sailor be given a Christian burial, and spent hours sitting in a driftwood hut on the cliffs, watching the sea, writing poetry and smoking opium. Hawker's Hut stands there to this day. Don't miss the Rectory Farm Tea Rooms nearby (☎ 01288 331251; www.rectory-tearooms.co.uk).

Centre above the village. ⏱ *3 hr. Nr Bideford, Devon EX39 5TA.* ☎ *01237 431781. www.clovelly. co.uk. Adult £5.75, child (ages 7–16) £3.65, family £15.50. Daily in summer 9am–6:30pm.*

⑥ Hartland Quay. Just across the Devon border, the evocative Hartland Peninsula is well worth a detour. Though little visited today, Hartland Quay was an important port in Georgian times, a welcome haven on a notoriously dangerous stretch of coastline. Eventually the harbour was destroyed by the ravages of the sea. The quayside Shipwreck Museum tells the stories of the many ships that have foundered on this coast. The lighthouse on Hartland Point was erected in 1874. ⏱ *1 hr.*

⑦ South West Coast Path. The stretch around Bude is one of the most dramatic anywhere along on the South West Coast Path. Geologically fascinating, the colourful cliff strata have been twisted and contorted, and jagged lines of rocks run at right angles into the sea. The steep terrain is hard going, and there are few places to get refreshment.

⑧ Widemouth Bay. A surfing hotspot. *See p 67.*

Where to **Stay & Dine**

★★ Camelot Hotel This comfortable, quiet hotel, first built as a private house in the 1920s has recently been refurbished. It overlooks the golf course and downs just inland from Crooklets Beach. Hawker's Restaurant is open to non-residents. *Downs View, Bude EX23 8RE.* ☎ *01288 352361.*

www.camelot-hotel.co.uk. 24 rooms. WiFi. £128 per room per night (dinner/ B&B packages available). MC, V.

★★★ Castle Restaurant An informal, bistro-style restaurant in a historic setting near the Bude Canal. Fixed-price express lunches;

frequently changing menus include much local, seasonal produce: grilled fish of the day, Holsworthy rump steak, primavera risotto, crab and parsnip linguini. *The Castle, The Wharf EX23 8LG.* ☎ *01288 350543. www.thecastlerestaurantbude. co.uk. Mains £14–17. MC, V. 10am–2:30pm, 6–9:30pm.*

★★ **Edgcumbe** An elegant, stylish B&B in a period house in one of the best locations in Bude, a quiet dead-end near Summerleaze Beach, with views towards the canal and sea-lock. Two rooms are classified as de luxe, with sea views; one has its own lounge. Downstairs, public areas include a bar, bistro and sun-lounge with sunset views. *Summerleaze Crescent EX23 8HJ.* ☎ *01288 353846. www.edgcumbe-hotel.co.uk. 12 rooms. WiFi. £34–47 pppn. MC, V.*

★★★ **Elements** Classy boutique-style accommodation and bistro dining (a terrace is outside) on the cliffs overlooking Widemouth Bay. The emphasis here is on local produce: fish from Bude Bay, meat from Bradworthy, Cornish fruit and veg, traditional Sunday lunches. A typical *menu du jour* might include: Devon cod, rump of lamb, Cornish crumbly cheese and fig chutney. There is a gymnasium, leisure facilities and 11 rooms. *Marine Drive, Widemouth Bay EX23 0LZ.* ☎ *01288 352386. www.elements-life.co.uk. Mains £11–17. MC, V. Daily 5–9:30pm, Sun midday–2:30pm.*

★★ **The Falcon Hotel** Built in 1798 as lodgings for visiting sea captains, this hotel claims to be the oldest coaching house in north Cornwall. The hotel and its walled

Ripe Café.

gardens overlook the Bude Canal (see ❷ above). Alfred Lord Tennyson stayed here in 1848 and broke his leg when he fell over the garden wall! The rooms are furnished to a high standard. Both the Falcon Inn and Tennyson's Restaurant specialise in local produce. *Breakwater Road EX23 8SD.* ☎ *01288 352005. www.falconhotel.com. 29 rooms. WiFi. £59–74 pppn. MC, V.*

★★ **Ripe Café** Cheerful, relaxed café where you can create your own breakfast (meat is free range, local and often rare breed); baked potatoes, panini, great homemade cakes, comfy chairs; children welcome. *2 Lansdown Road EX23 8BH.* ☎ *01288 355325. Mains ca. £5.75. MC, V, AmEx. Low season Mon–Sat 9am–5pm, Sun 10am–4pm; high season the same plus 6–9:30pm.*

Falmouth

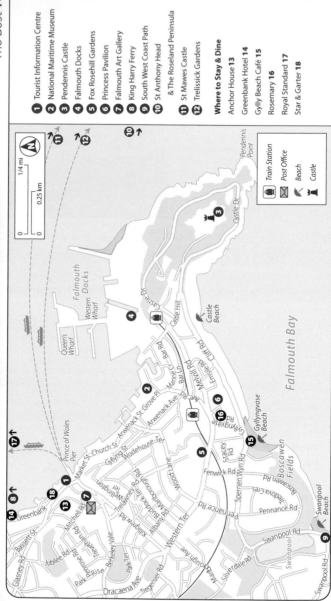

1 Tourist Information Centre
2 National Maritime Museum
3 Pendennis Castle
4 Falmouth Docks
5 Fox Rosehill Gardens
6 Princess Pavilion
7 Falmouth Art Gallery
8 King Harry Ferry
9 South West Coast Path
10 St Anthony Head
   & The Roseland Peninsula
11 St Mawes Castle
12 Trelissick Gardens

Where to Stay & Dine
Anchor House 13
Greenbank Hotel 14
Gylly Beach Café 15
Rosemary 16
Royal Standard 17
Star & Garter 18

Train Station
Post Office
Beach
Castle

Falmouth Bay

Falmouth Docks
Western Wharf
Queen's Wharf
Prince of Wales Pier
Castle Dr
Pendennis Point

Castle Beach
Castle Hill

Gyllyngvase Beach
Swanpool Beach
Boscawen Fields

Falmouth stands on the Carrick Roads, one of the world's largest natural deep-water harbours. The town combines the roles of tourist destination and working port. Until the 17th century, Falmouth was no more than a modest market town, but its fortunes prospered when Sir John Killigrew established a small port here. In 1689, the Falmouth Packet Service was set up, taking advantage of the port's southwesterly position and easy access to the open sea. Sailing ships carried post around the world until 1850. Commercial docks were built in 1860, and the railway arrived in 1863, heralding the tourist industry. Since the National Maritime Museum opened in 2002, Falmouth has undergone extensive regeneration.

Flushing, seen from Greenbank.

❶ Tourist Information Centre. *11 Market Strand, Prince of Wales Pier TR11 3DF.* ☎ *01326 312000. www.acornishriver.co.uk.*

❷ National Maritime Museum. *See p 38.*

❸ Pendennis Castle. *See p 58.*

Little Dennis Blockhouse. Situated off Castle Drive, this Tudor gun platform was used to attack enemy ships sailing close inshore.

Crab Quay Battery. This early 18th-century fortification contains the remains of a quay, a magazine (artillery store) and guardhouse.

❹ Falmouth Docks. Set on one of the world's busiest commercial seaways, Falmouth is an important shipbuilding and repair centre. A large lay-by on Castle Drive gives good views of the Carrick Roads, full of huge container ships.

❺ Fox Rosehill Gardens and **❻ Princess Pavilion.** Encouraged by the mild climate, beautiful gardens abound in this part of Cornwall (p 58): Fox Rosehill (lemon and banana trees) on Melvil Road, and Princess Pavilion behind Gyllyngvase Beach are worth a visit.

❼ Falmouth Art Gallery. This gallery, housed in the late 19th century Passmore Edwards Library, has one of Cornwall's finest collections of 20th-century art. ⏱ *2 hr. Municipal Buildings, The Moor TR11 2RT.* ☎ *01326 313863. www. falmouthartgallery.com. Free admission. Mon–Sat 10am–5pm.*

Places of Interest Nearby

8 King Harry Ferry. This chain-driven service began operating across the upper reaches of the Fal in 1888. The crossing (every 20 minutes) takes a matter of minutes, shaving large chunks off the long road route via Truro. *See p 157.*

9 South West Coast Path. The path west of Falmouth runs past St Dennis Head and the secluded church of St Anthony-in-Meneague before reaching the sheltered Helford estuary, a popular spot for sailing and the setting of Daphne du Maurier's novel *Frenchman's Creek* (p 107). To follow the path eastwards, take a ferry to the Roseland Peninsula (p 155).

10 St Anthony Head & The Roseland Peninsula. A lighthouse has guarded St Anthony Head since 1834, but before that a beacon warned sailors of the perils of the Manacles reef offshore. St Anthony Battery dates from the 19th century, with fortifications added in World War II. The battery and lighthouse now provide atmospheric holiday accommodation. The 13th-century church at St Just-in-Roseland has a truly idyllic setting, often used for TV and film location shots. ⏱ *1 hr. www. roselandpeninsula.info.*

11 St Mawes Castle. *See p 58.*

12 Trelissick Gardens. *See p 28.*

Where to **Stay & Dine**

★★★ **Anchor House** With brilliant views of the Carrick Roads, this quiet Victorian terrace offers comfortable B&B (with parking and a pretty courtyard garden). The interior is simple and tasteful. An open-plan lounge and breakfast room on the first floor makes the most of the view. Evening meals/packed lunches are available on request. Long-established, knowledgeable owner. *17 Harbour Terrace TR11 2AN.* ☎*01326 317006. www.anchorhouse falmouth.co.uk. 2 rooms. Broadband available. From £25 pppn. No credit cards.*

★★★ **Greenbank Hotel** Beside the Royal Cornwall Yacht Club on the edge of town, the recently refurbished Greenbank offers luxurious accommodation in an enviable waterfront position. The Riverside Restaurant specialises in local fish and meat, and the terrace has some of the best views in town. *Harbourside TR11 2SR.* ☎ *01326 312440. www.greenbank-hotel.co.uk. 59 rooms. WiFi. £79 (single)–199 (double) per room per night. MC, V.*

★★★ **Gylly Beach Café** Bang on the beach, this trendy, eco-friendly café/restaurant/bar serves summer Sunday BBQs at 6pm and tempting food all year round: Gylly burger with Cornish blue topping, curried sweet potato and chick pea cakes, crayfish sandwiches, tapas, dips, brownies, cream teas: unmissable. *Cliff Road TR11 4PA.* ☎ *01326 312884. www. gyllybeach.com. Mains: lunch £4.25–8.25, evening £8–14.50. MC, V. Daily 9am–at least 10pm.*

★★ **Rosemary** Just a few minutes' walk from Gyllyngvase Beach,

Take to the Water

By far the most enjoyable way of getting to central Falmouth is by water. As well as a year-round 'Park and Ride' bus service, a **'Park and Float'** runs from Ponsharden to Custom House Quay, late May–late Sept Mon–Fri. Go in by boat and return (free) by bus (☎ 01872 861910; www.falriverlinks.co.uk). For information on ferries in the area: **King Harry Ferry** (p 157) (☎ 01872 862312; www.kingharryscornwall.co.uk); **St Mawes Ferry** (Falmouth to St Mawes) (☎ 01872 861910; www.stmawsferry.co.uk); **Place Ferry** (Falmouth to Place Creek on the Roseland Peninsula) (☎ 01872 861910); **Enterprise Boats** (Falmouth to Truro and Malpas) (p 138); **Helford River Boats** (Helford estuary, including Glendurgan and Trebah Gardens; p 30 (☎ 01326 250770; www.helford-river-boats.co.uk).

this licensed guest house offers quiet, comfortable accommodation in a pretty Victorian house with off-road parking, south-facing garden and sundeck. All bedrooms have views over Falmouth Bay. *22 Gyllyngvase Terrace TR11 4DL.* ☎ *01326 314669. www.therosemary.co.uk. 8 rooms, including family suites. WiFi. £35–42 pppn. MC, V.*

★★ **Royal Standard**   A nicely updated but traditional village pub (wooden floors and furnishings, nautical knick-knacks, gentle music and a lovely sun terrace) with excellent food such as pork belly with creamy mash, smoked mackerel and prawn fishcakes, as well as delicious platters of local cheeses, fish and meats in high summer. Take the ferry from Falmouth (Prince of Wales Pier). *1 St Peter's Hill, Flushing TR11 5TP.* ☎ *01326 374250. Mains £5.25–10.50. MC, V. Summer Mon–Fri midday–11:30pm, from 8:30am Sat & Sun; winter Mon–Fri midday–3pm, 6–11.30pm, Sat & Sun midday–11:30pm.*

★★★ **Star & Garter**   This traditional and characterful local pub has

no outside seating, but superb waterfront views. It has a well-deserved reputation for good food: grilled seabass with tomato, butter-bean and chorizo stew; whole king prawns with garlic and Pernod cream sauce; local pork and leek sausages. *High Street TR11 2 AD.* ☎ *01326 318313. Mains £6.95–11.95. MC, V. Daily midday–11pm, Sun to 10:30pm.*

Custom House Quay.

Fowey

1. Tourist Information Centre
2. St Catherine's Castle
3. St Fimbarrus Church
4. Old House of Foye
5. Fowey & Polruan Blockhouses
6. Fowey Aquarium & Fowey Museum
7. Hall Walk
8. Castle Dore
9. Charlestown
10. Mevagissey

11. South West Coast Path

Where to Stay & Dine

Bistro 12
Food for Thought 13
King of Prussia 14
Marina Villa Hotel 15
Pinky Murphy's Boathouse Café 16
Trevanion Guest House 17

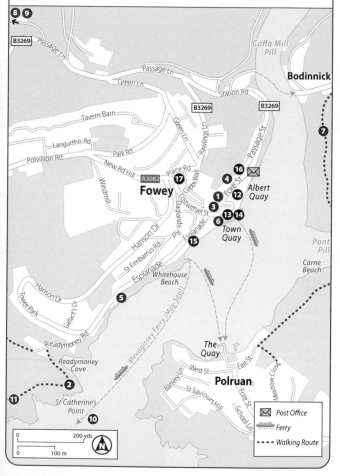

The old port of Fowey is a delightful jumble of narrow, hilly lanes, zigzagging via steps and terraces to an alluring waterfront. It's crammed with interesting shops and good places to eat. Popular with both tourists and leisure mariners, Fowey is still a working port, and china clay is exported from the docks upriver. Fowey took over Lostwithiel's role as a port in the 15th century when the river silted up (p 117). Catch the ferry to the old fishing village of Polruan, which still has an active boatyard. Both places are best explored on foot: a bus runs every 15 minutes from Fowey's main car park to St Fimbarrus Church (reduced service November to Easter).

❶ Tourist Information Centre. In the same building as the Daphne du Maurier Literary Centre (see box on p 107). *5 South Street PL23 1AR.* ☎ *01726 833616. www.fowey. co.uk.*

❷ St Catherine's Castle. *See p 61.*

❸ St Fimbarrus Church. St Fimbarrus marks the southern terminus of the Saints' Way (p 74). The mainly 15th-century church is dedicated to the Irish saint Finn Barr, a 7th-century bishop of Cork, said to have visited Fowey en route to Rome. It has a splendid porch and fine memorials to the Rashleighs of Menabilly, which later became Daphne du Maurier's home (p 107). ⏲ *30 min. www. foweyparishchurch.org.*

❹ Old House of Foye. This medieval house, the oldest in Fowey, dates from around 1430. *Fore Street.* ⏲ *5 min. Not open to the public.*

❺ Fowey & Polruan Blockhouses. Fowey harbour is flanked by two late 14th-century blockhouses, one in Fowey and the opposite at Polruan. Chains were suspended across the harbour for the protection against invading ships. Catch the ferry to Polruan to have a closer look; the Fowey blockhouse is closed to visitors. ⏲ *30 min.*

❻ Fowey Aquarium & Fowey Museum are both housed in the 15th-century Town Hall. ⏲ *1½ hr.*

View of Fowey from Polruan.

Town Hall, Trafalgar Square. ☎ *01726 833516. Museum 10:30am–5pm Mon–Fri Easter–mid Oct; aquarium open in summer. Admission £1.*

❼ Hall Walk. Established in the 16th-century, this scenic route leads from Bodinnick to Penleath Point on the east bank of the Fowey, where King Charles I was fired upon in 1644. A memorial to the Cornish writer and local resident, Sir Arthur Quiller-Couch [1863–1944], stands on the site. ⏲ *1–1½ hr.*

Places of Interest Nearby
❽ Castle Dore. Find a parking space (not easy) on the busy B3269

Mevagissey harbour.

and walk to Castle Dore; access is permitted by the owner (no formal right of way). This well-preserved Iron Age settlement consists of a circular rampart within an oval one, protecting about 20 round houses; a Civil War battle took place nearby in 1644. ⏱ *30 min.*

9 Charlestown. This Georgian port, built between 1790 and 1810 for the export of copper and china clay, remains little changed; tall ships rise high above the water and beautiful Georgian houses overlook the harbour. This is a frequently-used film location. ⏱ *1½ hr. TIC.* ☎ *01726 879500. www.cornish-riviera.co.uk.*

10 Mevagissey. A ferry runs from Fowey to the immensely popular fishing port Mevagissey in summer, a lovely trip across St Austell Bay. Mevagissey has long been an important fishing port: the first pier here was built in the 15th century. ⏱ *1 day. TIC.* ☎ *01726 844440. www. mevagissey-cornwall.co.uk.*

11 South West Coast Path. The path to the east of Fowey passes St Catherine's Castle (p 61) and then drops to Polridmouth, overlooked by a manorial corn mill on the Menabilly estate the inspiration for Du Maurier's Manderley (see box on p 107). On Gribben Head farther along stands the red-and-white striped Gribbin Tower, a daymark erected by Trinity House in 1832.

Where to **Stay & Dine**

★★★ **Bistro** Relaxed, good service amid whitewashed walls and photos of local landscapes. Most ingredients are sourced locally: roast fillet of cod, Treesmill rump of lamb, Tregida smoked haddock risotto; irresistible puddings. The downstairs bar is for non-diners. *24 Fore Street PL23 1AQ.* ☎ *01726 832322. www.tiffinsdeli.co.uk. 2 courses £12.95–19.95, 3 courses £15.95–24.95. MC, V. Daily 10am–5:30pm (not Wed), Thurs–Mon 6–11pm.*

★★ **Food for Thought** This restaurant is perfectly located on the quay, in a fascinating medieval building (possibly a merchant's

Daphne du Maurier

The novelist Daphne du Maurier (1907–89) introduced Cornwall to untold thousands of admirers. Her love affair with Fowey began during childhood visits to her family's holiday home at Bodinnick. In adulthood, she settled permanently in Cornwall. She married in Lanteglos church (p 150), and lived first at Readymoney Cove and then at Menabilly, ancestral seat of the Rashleigh family and the inspiration for Manderley, before moving to Kilmarth, a mile away. Her most famous novels *Jamaica Inn*, *Frenchman's Creek* and *Rebecca* capture the spirit of Cornwall as few other writers have. Fowey hosts the Daphne du Maurier Festival in May each year (www.dumaurierfestival.co.uk).

house) with inside/outside seating. The menu majors on fish – dressed crab, moules mariniere and salmon – but there are other dishes too, such as roasted pig with crackling. *Town Quay PL23 1AT.* ☎ *01726 832221. www.foodforthoughtfowey. com. Dinner fixed price £19.95 (Mon–Fri excl. Bank Hols). Mains (dinner) £14.95–21.95. No credit cards. Mon–Sat 7–9:30pm.*

★★ King of Prussia A historic building and popular pub, the 'King of Prussia' was the nickname for the notorious smuggler John Carter (1770–1807). The rooms have recently been well refurbished; all have big windows with river views – perfect for watching the world go by. Four have sofabeds and can accommodate families. *3 Town Quay PL23 1AT.* ☎ *01726 833694. 6 rooms. Summer £45 pppn, winter* **B** *35 pppn. No cedit cards.*

★★★ Marina Villa Hotel A stay at the Michelin-starred Marina is recommended for foodies. This boutique hotel, in a Georgian town house, is now a gourmet destination under chef Nathan Outlaw (seven-course tasting menu). Some rooms have private balconies; one is on its own in the waterside garden.

Esplanade PL23 1HY. ☎ *01726 833315. www.themarinahotel.co.uk. 18 rooms. WiFi. From £164 double room. No credit cards.*

★★ Pinky Murphy's Boat-house Café This small, cosy place is full of brightly coloured cushions and shells and interesting odds and ends. There is a small outside seating area, and a spacious room upstairs. The food is as much fun as the café: platters of humus, pesto, ham, salami; pains au choco-lats, chocolate brownies, muffins and homemade cakes. *19 North Street PL23 1DB.* ☎ *01726 832512. www.pinkymurphys.com. Mains £4.50–7.95. No credit cards. Mon–Sat 9am–5ish, Sun 9:30–4ish.*

★★ Trevanion Guest House Wake to the sound of seagulls and lovely views over the rooftops. This comfortable guesthouse in a historic building uphill from the church can accommodate families and has parking, as well as very good break-fasts: free-range eggs, homemade jams and marmalade. *70 Lostwithiel Street PL23 1BQ.* ☎ *01726 832602. www.trevanionguesthouse.co.uk. 5 rooms. WiFi. £50–80 per room per night. No credits cards.*

Launceston

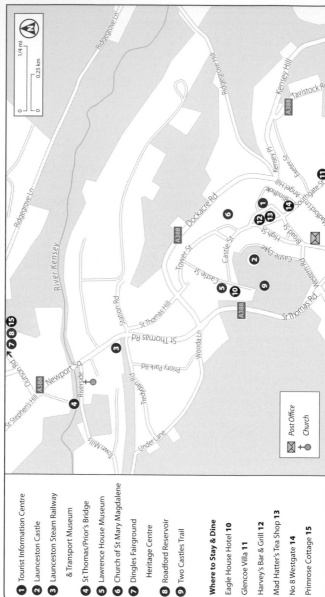

1/4 mi

0.25 km

Ridgegrove Ln

Kensey Hill

Tavistock Rd

A388

Kensey Pl

Exeter St

Ridgegrove Ln

River Kensey

Ridgegrove Ln

Dockacre Rd

A388

Madford Ln

St Aug's Hill

Angel Hill

Windmill

Castle Dyke

High St

Broad St

1

12 13

14

11

6

Castle St

Tower St

Castle St

2

Westgate St

Castle Dyke

Station Rd

5 10

9

St Thomas Hill

A388

St Thomas Rd

St Stephen's Hill

Dutson Rd

A388

Newport Sq

St Thomas Rd

St Thomas Hill

Wooda Ln

3

Riverside

Tredydan Rd

Priory Park Rd

Under Lane

Town Mills

4

Post Office

Church

1 Tourist Information Centre
2 Launceston Castle
3 Launceston Steam Railway
  & Transport Museum
4 St Thomas/Prior's Bridge
5 Lawrence House Museum
6 Church of St Mary Magdalene
7 Dingles Fairground
  Heritage Centre
8 Roadford Reservoir
9 Two Castles Trail

Where to Stay & Dine

Eagle House Hotel **10**

Glencoe Villa **11**

Harvey's Bar & Grill **12**

Mad Hatter's Tea Shop **13**

No 8 Westgate **14**

Primrose Cottage **15**

Most people miss this historic town as they race across the Devon border on the A30. But Launceston is well worth a visit: it was Cornwall's capital until 1835 and is the only walled town in the county. It grew up on a hilltop site around a well-preserved medieval core (the South Gate is the only surviving original gateway). Notice the carved wooden quarterjacks on the Guildhall's clock tower, which emerge to strike every quarter hour. The castle was founded in the 11th century and remodelled two centuries later. In 1656 George Fox, founder of the Society of Friends, or Quakers, was imprisoned in the North Gate for 8 months for disturbing the peace by distributing leaflets.

Launceston Castle.

1 Tourist Information Centre.

Pick up a historic town trail leaflet. *Market House Arcade, Market Street PL15 78EP.* ☎ *01566 772321. www. visitlaunceston.co.uk.*

2 Launceston Castle. *See p 63.*

3 Launceston Steam Railway & Transport Museum.

Take a trip along part of the old Launceston & South Devon Railway behind a Victorian narrow-gauge steam engine. The original track ran to Padstow between 1865 and 1962. Today the ride (in open or closed carriages, depending on the weather) runs for 2½ miles (4km)

along the Kensey Valley to New Mills Farm Park (☎ *01566 777106; www. newmillsfarmpark.com).* ⏱ *3 hr. St Thomas Road PL15 8DA.* ☎ *01566 775665. www.launcestonsr.co.uk. Adult return £8.25, child (ages 3–15) £5.50, concessions £6.50, family £25. Trains hourly early Apr–end Sept & Oct half-term 11am–4pm (daily except Sat in peak season).*

4 St Thomas/Prior's Bridge.

This medieval footbridge once linked the Priory (an Augustinian monastery founded in 1126, which fell into ruin after the Dissolution of the monasteries under Henry VIII's reign) with its tenants in Newport. Riverside. ⏱ *10 min.*

5 Lawrence House Museum.

Castle Street was said by Sir John Betjeman (p 126) to be the finest Georgian street in Cornwall. Lawrence House was built in 1753. It served as a billet for prisoners of war during the Napoleonic wars and now contains a local history museum. ⏱ *2 hr. 9 Castle Street PL15 8BA.* ☎ *01566 773277. www. lawrencehousemuseum.org.uk. Free admission. End Mar–end Oct Mon–Fri 10:30–4:30pm.*

6 Church of St Mary Magdalene.

The earliest church on this site was built in 1080, around the same time as the castle. Only the tower survives of a second church,

Church of St Mary Magdalene.

dating from 1380. The present church was built by Henry Trecarrell in memory of his infant son, who drowned in 1511; the work took 13 years. Its granite exterior is intricately carved with foliage and heraldic designs. ⏲ *30 min.*

Places of Interest Nearby
7 Dingles Fairground Heritage Centre. This wonderfully quirky place entertains children of all ages with steam engines, vintage vehicles, weird and wonderful agricultural machines (including an apple peeler), late 19th-century fairground rides (some in working order) and other fairground memorabilia. ⏲ *3 hr. Lifton, Devon PL16 0AT.* ☎ *01566 783425. www.fairground-heritage.org. uk. Adult £7, child (ages 3–16) £5, family £21, concessions £5. Mid-Mar–end Oct Thurs–Mon 10:30am–5:30pm; all week during school summer holidays.*

8 Roadford Reservoir. Construction began in 1989, and today the reservoir provides an excellent range of amenities. You can go camping, sailing, windsurfing, rowing, kayaking or canoeing, enjoy a leisurely stroll along walking trails, try your hand at fishing, learn more about the reservoir at the visitor centre or enjoy a meal at the lakeside restaurant. *Lower Goodacre, Broadwoodwidger, Lifton, Devon PL16 0JL.* ☎ *01409 211507. www. swlakestrust.org.uk. Restaurant: 11am–5pm in season, phone for winter opening times.*

9 Two Castles Trail. A 24-mile (38km) walking route linking the castles at Launceston and Okehampton in Devon, this is an excellent way to explore the river valleys, ridge roads, open downland and woods on the peaceful Cornwall/Devon border. Okehampton Castle (owned by English Heritage), one of the largest in the county, was the seat of the Earls of Devon in medieval times. ⏲ *2 days. www.devon.gov.uk.*

Where to **Stay & Dine**

★★ **Eagle House Hotel** In the oldest, quietest part of town by the castle walls, this elegant hotel was built as a gentleman's residence in 1764. It has off-street parking and gardens. *3 Castle Street PL15 8BA.* ☎ *01566 772036. www.eaglehousse hotel.eu. 13 rooms. WiFi. £68–75 per room per night. MC, V.*

★★ **Glencoe Villa** This comfortable, homely B&B in a Victorian hilltop house has lovely views over the Tamar Valley and lies just a short walk from the town's historic heart.

Guests can use the terrace and garden, and there's parking. *13 Race Hill PL15 9BB.* ☎ *01566 775819. 3 rooms. £25–45 pppn. No credit cards.*

★★ Harvey's Bar & Grill

A lively, modern eating place in the heart of Launceston offering excellent food: Cornish beef and sausages, wild mushroom stroganoff, Sunday roasts and breakfast from 10am: has specials nights, live music and takeaways midday– 2pm, 6–9pm. *13 Church Street PL15 8AW.* ☎ *01566 772558. www. bar13launceston. co.uk. Mains £5.50– 9.95. MC, V. Mon–Thurs 10am–1pm, Fri–Sun 10am–midnight.*

★★ Mad Hatter's Tea Shop   A

traditional teashop offering over 50 different teas, including Gunpowder Green, Russian Caravan, rosehip and

hibiscus. The owners collect and sell teapots of all shapes and sizes. Good-value lunches and teas: huge scones, Cornish fairings and delicious Launceston cake, made from an ancient recipe. *28 Church Street PL15 8AR.* ☎ *01566 774634. www.the-mad hatters.co.uk. Mains £3.15– 5.65. MC, V. Mon–Sat 9:30am–4:30pm.*

★★ No 8 Westgate   This

licensed café/coffee bar is just off Launceston's main square, with comfy modern furnishings, several spacious dining areas and a covered verandah. It provides a good range of salads and light snacks (panini, pasta dishes, tapas, nachos, etc.), plus tempting cakes, puds and drinks. *8 Westgate PL15 8AR.* ☎ *01566 777369. Mains £6.25–6.95. MC, V. Mon–Sat 8:30am– 5pm; longer hours & early evenings in summer.*

★★★ Primrose Cottage   A

touch of luxury in a lovely setting on the Devon–Somerset border 4 miles (6½km) south of Launceston. The cottage dates from the 18th century, but has been tastefully extended to provide three private suites, each with a sitting room. The gardens are a wildlife haven, and paths lead to down to riverside meadows. Light suppers available with 24 hours notice). *Lawhitton, Launceston PL15 9PE.* ☎ *01566 773645. www.primrosecottage suites.co.uk. 3 suites. £55–65 pppn. MC, V.*

Mad Hatter's Tea Shop sign.

The Eagle House Hotel.

Looe

1 Tourist Information Centre
2 Old Guildhall Museum & Gaol
3 Sarah's Pasty Shop
4 Looe Island (St George's Island)
5 Looe Valley Line
6 Liskeard
7 Monkey Sanctuary Trust
8 Paul Corin's Magnificent Music Machines
9 Polperro
10 South West Coast Path

Where to Stay & Dine

Golden Guinea Restaurant 11
Hannafore Point Hotel 12
Old Bridge House 13
Pier Café & Terrace 14
Squid Ink Restaurant 15
Tidal Court 16
Trenderway Farm 17

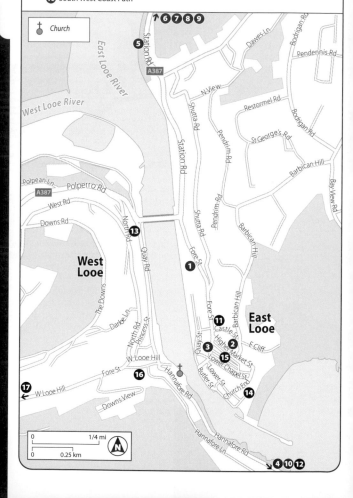

The south coast port of Looe developed where two rivers meet, just before flowing into Looe Bay. Originally the settlements that grew up on either bank were quite separate, but a bridge connected them from 1436 onwards. East Looe is the main seaside town, with the harbour and a popular sandy beach. Shops, eating places and historic buildings line its quaint medieval streets, attracting thousands of visitors in summer. West Looe is a quieter residential zone with headland walks to Hannafore, overlooking Looe Island. Looe is a thriving deep-sea port with a daily fish market. It specialises in shark fishing and boat trips are advertised at Buller Quay.

Looe harbour.

❶ Tourist Information Centre. Below the clock tower; pick up a heritage town trail leaflet. *The Guildhall, Fore Street, East Looe.* ☎ 01503 262072. www.looe.org & www.visit-southeastcornwall.co.uk.

❷ Old Guildhall Museum & Gaol. The Guildhall is Looe's oldest building, a former courthouse dating from 1500 (the original bench is still in place). A new Guildhall replaced it in Victorian times and its predecessor now houses the Old Guildhall Museum, tracing Looe's history as a shipbuilding and fishing centre. 🕐 *1½ hr. Higher Market Street, East Looe PL13 1BP.* ☎ 01503 263709. *Daily end May–end Sept 11:30am–4:30pm (not Sat except Bank Hols).*

❸ Sarah's Pasty Shop. One of the best pasty makers in Cornwall – not to be missed! *Buller Street.*

❹ Looe Island (St George's Island). A notorious haunt of smugglers in the 18th century, Looe Island lies about 1 mile (1½km) off Hannafore Point. For many years it was owned and inhabited by two sisters, Evelyn and Babs Atkins, who bequeathed it to the Cornwall Wildlife Trust in 2004. The island is now

Sarah's Pasty Shop.

a marine nature reserve open to day visitors (regular boat service in summer; take your own refreshments). ⏲ *1 day. All year round, and weather depending. www.looe island.co.uk & www.cornwallwildlife trust.org.uk.*

⑤ Looe Valley Line. A delightful 8¾-mile (14km) railway journey through the wooded Looe Valley. The Rail Ale Trail visits a number of pubs along the way; a booklet 'Trails from the Track' suggests local walks. ⏲ *30 min. www.looevalley walking.com & www.railaletrail.com.*

Places of Interest Nearby
⑥ Liskeard. This ancient market town at the head of the Looe Valley received its first charter in 1240, and became one of Cornwall's four stannary towns (where tin was weighed and taxed). Many Victorian buildings survive, including the Town Hall, Guild Hall and Clock Tower. The Pipe Well is thought to possess miraculous healing powers for 'weak eyes'. Don't miss Gwynn

ha Du, the Cornish shop in Fore Street, and Taste of Cornwall, an excellent specialist food shop on Bay Tree Hill. ⏲ *2 hr. www.liskeard. gov.uk.*

⑦ Monkey Sanctuary Trust. *See p 152.*

⑧ Paul Corin's Magnificent Music Machines. A quirky, nostalgic collection of music machines (in full working order). The highlight is the Mighty Wurlitzer Theatre Organ, a kind of 'one-man orchestra'. ⏲ *2 hr. St Keyne Station, Liskeard PL14 4SH.* ☎ *01579 343108. Adult £5.50, child £2.50, family £14, concessions £5. Daily Easter–end Oct 10:30am–5:30pm.*

⑨ Polperro. *See p 150.*

⑩ South West Coast Path. Beyond Hannafore Point the path west of Looe leads to the lovely Talland Bay (where there are two very good cafés), and the ancient church of St Tallanus.

Historic Liskeard.

Where to **Stay & Dine**

★ Golden Guinea Restaurant

One of Looe's most historic buildings, where a £10,000 hoard of golden guineas was once found in a cupboard. Good quality traditional down-to-earth fare: roasts, steaks, mixed grill, king prawns and salads plus a children's menu. *Fore Street, East Looe PL13 1AD.* ☎ *01503 262780. Mains £7.35–14.95. MC, V. Daily 10:30am–9:30/10pm.*

★★ Hannafore Point Hotel

A big, luxury hotel in a quiet waterfront position in West Looe. Facilities include an indoor leisure spa and swimming pool. There are spacious, sea-view rooms with balconies; a children's activity programme in summer; lots of activities arranged such as sailing, diving, deep-sea fishing and other boat trips, golf and tennis. *Marine Drive, Hannafore, West Looe PL13 2DG.* ☎ *01503 263273. www.hannaforepointhotel.com. 37 rooms. WiFi. £42–92 dinner, B&B pppn. MC, V.*

★★ Old Bridge House

Handily close to the bridge, this welcoming licensed B&B provides comfortable, practical accommodation. The rooms aren't large, but are light and nicely furnished. there is a small guest lounge and honesty bar, and a small terrace with river views; no on-site parking (public parking is nearby). *The Quay, West Looe PL13 2BU.* ☎ *01503 263159. www.theold bridgehouse.com. 9 rooms. WiFi. £34–49 pppn. MC, V.*

★ Pier Café & Terrace

A bright, clean, cheerful café (open kitchen) just behind Town Beach, which is great for breakfasts, snacks and lunches: baked potatoes, ciabatta, salads, cream teas, cakes and a children's menu, plus Roskilly's ice cream (p 159). It has a large attractive indoor seating area and outside tables. *Seafront, East Looe PL13 1BX.* ☎ *01503 269147. Mains £3.25–5.95. No credit cards. Daily early Apr–end Oct 9am–6pm-ish.*

★★ Squid Ink Restaurant

This chef-owned restaurant in East Looe's historic heart features gourmet British cooking with Mediterranean and Asian influences, using local fish. Dishes include: fillet of Looe dayboat fish with Fowey mussels; panfried fillet of seabass; roast butternut squash with goat's cheese; tagliatelle nero (black ribbon pasta flavoured with squid ink). *Lower Chapel Street, East Looe PL13 1AT.* ☎ *01503 262674. www.squid-ink.biz. Mains £15.25–18.95. MC, V. Easter–Sept Wed–Sat & Nov–Jan Thurs–Sat lunch midday, dinner 6–9pm; private dining all year by arrangement.*

★ Tidal Court

A cosy, old-fashioned little B&B tucked away in West Looe's old fish shop; the building dates back 600 years. The accommodation is on three floors (with stairs and narrow passageways), and all rooms have fridges. *3 Church Street, West Looe PL13 2EX.* ☎ *01503 263695. 5 rooms. £25 pppn. No credit cards.*

★★★ Trenderway Farm

High-quality B&B accommodation in a 16th-century working farm away from the bustle of Looe (no children accepted). Accommodation is in the main house or converted farm buildings (two suites with 'kitchoos' –mini kitchens). An idyllic place to stay with spacious, beautifully furnished rooms, gourmet breakfasts and a library. *Polperro PL13 2LY.* ☎ *01503 272214. www.trenderwayfarm.com. 6 rooms. WiFi. £95–165 per room per night. MC, V.*

Lostwithiel

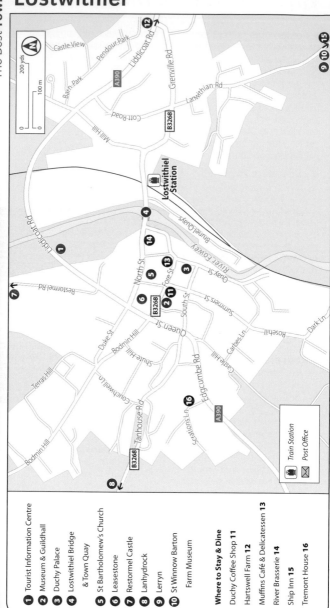

Castle View
Pendour Park
Barn Park
A390
Liddicoat Rd
Grenville Rd
Lanwithian Rd
Cott Road
Mill Hill
B3268
Lostwithiel Station
Liddicoat Rd
Brunel Quays
RIVER FOWEY
Restormel Rd
North St
Quay St
Fore St
Summers St
Duke St
Bodmin Hill
Shute Hill
Queen St
South St
Carbes Ln
Rosehill
Dark Ln
Terras Hill
Couchwell Ln
Tanhouse Rd
Castle Hill
Edgcumbe Rd
Scrations Ln
A390
Bodmin Hill
B3268

200 yds
100 m

1. Tourist Information Centre
2. Museum & Guildhall
3. Duchy Palace
4. Lostwithiel Bridge
   & Town Quay
5. St Bartholomew's Church
6. Leasestone
7. Restormel Castle
8. Lanhydrock
9. Lerryn
10. St Winnow Barton
    Farm Museum

Where to Stay & Dine

Duchy Coffee Shop **11**

Hartswell Farm **12**

Muffins Café & Delicatessen **13**

River Brasserie **14**

Ship Inn **15**

Tremont House **16**

Train Station
Post Office

Lostwithiel was the county capital in the 13th century, and it's still well worth stopping to explore this small, historic market town on the upper reaches of the River Fowey. Until the river silted, Lostwithiel was an important inland port and, like Liskeard, a stannary town in medieval times, authorised to assay tin from the local mines. Today, the town's medieval and Georgian streets are packed with antique shops, craft shops and good places to eat. Crowning a hill to the north is the evocative ruin of Restormel Castle.

❶ Tourist Information Centre. The TIC is clearly signed off the A390. You can pick up a copy of the town walks booklet here. *Community Centre, Liddicoat Road PL22 0HE. ☎ 01208 872207. www. lostwithieltic.org.uk.*

❷ Museum & Guildhall. Built in 1740, the ground floor of the building served as a corn market until the end of the 19th century and now houses the town museum. The Guildhall is on the upper storey. 🕐 *1 hr. 16 Fore Street PL22 0AS. ☎ 01208 872079. Free admission. Easter–end Sept 10:30am–12:30pm, 2:30–4:30pm.*

❸ Duchy Palace. This 13th-century building formed part of the Shire Hall. The Dukedom (Duchy) of Cornwall was created in 1337 to provide an independent income for the heir to the throne, a tradition that continues to this day. The Palace is part of a complex of buildings where the tin industry was regulated; the Stannary (the tinners') Parliament was held here from the 14th century until it was discontinued in 1752. The next building along Quay Street houses the Stannary prison (look for the narrow barred windows on the top storey): this was the Stannary prison. In 2009, restoration work began on the Duchy Palace, funded by The Prince's Regeneration Trust (www. princes-regeneration.org). *Not open to the public. Junction of Fore and Quay Streets.*

❹ Lostwithiel Bridge & Town Quay. Take a stroll down to the

Lostwithiel Bridge.

'History in every stone. . .'

The poet laureate Sir John Betjeman (p 126) is reputed to have said 'There is history in every stone in Lostwithiel'. The town enjoyed enormous prestige in the late 13th century when Restormel Castle (1 mile [1½km] to the north [p 61]) was rebuilt for Edmund, Earl of Cornwall.

Poet John Betjeman's grave, St Enodoc Church at Trebetherick.

riverside. In medieval times, when sea-going vessels could reach Lostwithiel, the Town Quay would have been a hive of activity. The first stone bridge was constructed in about 1300, replacing an earlier wooden one. It has been extended and repaired over the years as the river's course has altered. ⏲ *10 min. Bottom of Fore Street and along Quay Street.*

❺ St Bartholomew's Church. Lostwithiel's parish church is built in

Historic Lostwithiel.

the Breton style and dedicated to the patron saint of tanners (tanning was an important local industry). The lantern tower dates from the 13th century, with the distinctive spire being added in the 14th. During the Civil War, the church was desecrated and used to stable horses. ⏲ *30 min.*

❻ Leasestone. This unusual carved stone can be found on the corner of the former malthouse on Malthouse Lane. It states that the building lease (which began in 1652) should run for 3,000 years. ⏲ *5 min.*

❼ Restormel Castle. *See p 61.*

Places of Interest Nearby
❽ Lanhydrock. *See p 60.*

❾ Lerryn. *See p 150.*

❿ St Winnow Barton Farm Museum. This barns houses a low-key but charming collection of farm implements close to St Winnow Church on one of the prettiest stretches of the River Fowey, 2 miles (3¼km) south of Lostwithiel. Part of St Winnow Church dates from Norman times; one of the bench-ends shows a medieval Cornishman swigging from a pint pot. *See p 149.*

Where to **Stay & Dine**

★ **Duchy Coffee Shop** A traditional licensed tearoom/café in an attractive late 17th-century building, with old drawings of Lostwithiel on the walls. Reasonably priced light meals: scrambled egg and smoked salmon, Duchy Breakfast, jacket potatoes – and not a chip in sight. *Fore Street PL22 0BW.* ☎ *01208 873184. Mains £4.90–5.90.No credit cards. Mon–Sat 10am–5pm, most Sun and Bank Hols from 11am.*

★★ **Hartswell Farm** This is a lovely, secluded 17th-century farmhouse offering comfortable B&B within easy reach of the A390 1 mile (1½km) east of Lostwithiel. It is a small working farm producing beef for market. Bird boxes and a farm trail will please wildlife fans. The name 'Hartswell' derives from the days when the local Boconnoc estate watered its deer herd at this site. *St Winnow PL22 0RB.* ☎ *01208 8734319. www.connexions.co.uk/ hartswell. 3 rooms. £24–36 pppn. No credit cards.*

★★★ **Muffins Café & Delicatessen** Award-winning tearoom specialising in all things Cornish: farmhouse cider, St Endellion brie, Tregida smoked mackerel, Menallack farmhouse cheddar, Deli Farm charcuterie and Treleavans ice cream. If you're finding it impossible to choose from the tempting menu, go for the Muffins taster plate. Spacious with a lovely garden. *32 Fore Street PL2 0BN.* ☎ *01208 872278 www.muffinsdeli. co.uk. Mains £5.25– 6.95. MC, V. Tues–Sat 10am–5pm & Mon in Aug.*

★★★ **River Brasserie** This tastefully decorated bar and restaurant, in an interesting blue-and-white painted building at the bottom of Fore Street, specialises in local produce, much of it sourced from Lostwithiel farmers' market: Cornish sirloin steak, Cornish crab, roast Cornish cod, butternut squash risotto. Booking recommended. *Parade Square PL22 0DX.* ☎ *01208 872774 www.riverbrasserie.co.uk. Mains £13–17. MC, V. Tues–Sat 6–9pm, closed Sun.*

★★ **Ship Inn** The peaceful village of Lerryn is a delightful spot, just a mile or so south of Lostwithiel. The Ship Inn dates from the 16th century and is remarkably unspoilt, with dark beams and slate floors. It has five rooms, two suitable for families, all of which can be accessed without going through the inn. The Ship specialises in real ales, and food is locally-sourced wherever possible. *Lerryn, nr Lostwithiel PL22 0PT.* ☎ *01208 8722374. www.the shipinnlerryn.co.uk. 5 rooms plus 2 self-catering cottages. MC, V. £45–55 pppn.*

★★ **Tremont House** This attractive Victorian villa, built in the late 1880s and retaining many original features, is conveniently near to the town centre. It has good-sized rooms, two suitable for families, and views over the town: Green Tourism Business Scheme Silver Award winner. *2 The Terrace PL22 0DT.* ☎ *01208 873055. www.tremonthouse. co.uk. 3 rooms. MC, V. £25–32.50 pppn.*

THE VERY BEST OF
Muffins
CORNISH PRODUCE
Lunches Teas Snacks

Muffins sign.

Newquay

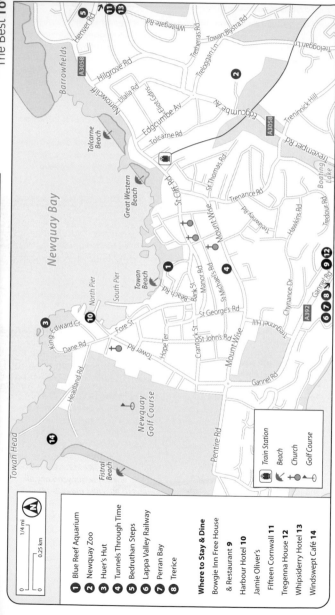

Blue Reef Aquarium **1**
Newquay Zoo **2**
Huer's Hut **3**
Tunnels Through Time **4**
Bedruthan Steps **5**
Lappa Valley Railway **6**
Perran Bay **7**
Trerice **8**

Where to Stay & Dine

Bowgie Inn Free House
& Restaurant **9**
Harbour Hotel **10**
Jamie Oliver's
Fifteen Cornwall **11**
Tregenna House **12**
Whipsiderry Hotel **13**
Windswept Café **14**

Train Station
Beach
Church
Golf Course

The UK's surfing capital isn't everyone's first choice of holiday destination. Newquay attracts hordes of young people over the summer months, and the population can hit 100,000. The irresistible draw is its magnificent beaches of fine blond sand, endlessly pounded by a drumroll of awesome Atlantic breakers. There's lots of cheap accommodation, including campsites, and the towns many hotels are popular with coach tours. It's certainly the place to go for nightlife. Many visitors prefer to stay nearby and use the town's facilities during the day rather than stay right in the centre. The harbour has some vestigial signs of Newquay's fishing port origins; the rest of town seems geared exclusively to the needs of its beach-boys and girls.

View of Newquay

Tourist Information

Marcus Hill, Newquay, Cornwall TR7 1BD, ☎ 01637 854020, email: newquay.tic@cornwall.gov.uk, www.visitnewquay.org.

❶ Blue Reef Aquarium. An excellent aquarium with over 40 themed habitats, from Cornish waters to subtropical seas, talks and feeding displays, the Blue Reef Nursery (captive breeding), Shark Lagoon, Turtle Creek and much, much more. A great day out for all ages. ⏱ *3 hr. Towan Beach TR7 1DU. ☎ 01637 787134. www.blue reefaquarium.co.uk. Adult £8.95, child (ages 3–14) £6.95, family £26, concessions £7.95. Daily 10am–5pm.*

❷ Newquay Zoo. This award-winning zoo and environmental park in lovely Trenance Gardens has daily talks and feeding times (a chance for close encounters) and an ongoing conservation programme. The zoo is run on eco-friendly lines and encourages visitors to arrive by train (using the Atlantic Coast Newquay–Par line). ⏱ *3 hr. Trenance Gardens TR7 2LZ. ☎ 01637 873342. www.newquayzoo.org.uk. Adult £10.95, child (ages 3–15) £8.20, family £32.90, concessions £8.25. Apr–end-Sept 9:30am–6pm, Oct–end-Mar 19am–5pm.*

❸ Huer's Hut. A reminder of the days when Newquay's main industry was pilchard fishing. The shore-based 'huers' used to alert the fishermen out in their boats about the location of shoals of pilchard, by shouting 'Hewa! Hewa!' from these lookout points. ⏱ *10 min. Harbour.*

④ Tunnels Through Time. A good place for a rainy day: an indoor, all-weather attraction that tells the story of Cornwall's legends, using realistic life-size figures. ⏱ *1½ hr. St Michael's Road.* ☎ *01637 873379. www.tunnelsthroughtime. Adult £4.40, child (ages 5–15) £2.20, family £12.80, concessions £3.30. Easter–Oct Sun–Fri 10am–5pm.*

Places of Interest Nearby
⑤ Bedruthan Steps. This popular beauty spot is a few miles north of Newquay and now in the hands of the National Trust. Cornish folklore says that the huge and eye-catching rocky stacks on the beach are stepping-stones, used by the Giant Bedruthan. Carnewas Tea-room by the car park is a handy spot to revive yourself if you take the long walk down to the beach and back again. ⏱ *2 hr.*

⑥ Lappa Valley Railway. *See p 39.*

⑦ Perran Bay. This beautiful sandy beach south of Newquay is said to be the landing place of St Piran, in the 6th century. Legend says that he was tied to a millstone and floated across the sea from Ireland to this spot on the north Cornish coast, where he built an oratory. ⏱ *2 hr to walk to the oratory and back. www.st-piran.com.*

⑧ Trerice. *See p 59.*

Where to **Stay & Dine**

★ **Bowgie Inn Free House & Restaurant** A big, efficient, if rather impersonal pub/restaurant on Pentire Head, with panoramic views over Crantock Beach. There's a huge car park and masses of outside seating, reflecting the pub's popularity in summer. Generous portions of pub food are served: steaks, salads, lasagne, Sunday roasts, and steak and kidney pie. Contains function rooms and Sky TV. *West Pentire, Crantock TR8 5RZ.* ☎ *01637 830363. www.bowgie. com. Mains £7–16.50; specials £10 max. MC, V. Daily 11am–11pm, Sun to 10:30pm.*

Newquay harbour: a quiet corner.

★★★ Harbour Hotel

Undeniably the most attractive, best situated and nicest small hotel in Newquay, overlooking the old harbour and hidden away in the quietest part of town, with easy access to Towan and Fistral beaches. This is a gem: all the rooms are tastefully decorated, with balconies overlooking the harbour. The restaurant (indoor and al fresco) specialises in local foods and the café is open from 10am daily. *North Quay Hill TR7 1HF.* ☎ *01637 873040. www.theharbour.co.uk. 5 rooms. WiFi. MC, V. £130–140 per room per night.*

Watergate Bay.

★★★ Jamie Oliver's Fifteen Cornwall

Founded by the celebrity chef in 2002 as part of an enterprise to help disadvantaged young people (in this case from Cornwall), Fifteen Cornwall offers an innovative Italian-inspired menu of the best local and seasonal produce in a stunning location. It's a great place to go for a special occasion – or treat yourself to breakfast overlooking the beach: pancakes, granola, smoked salmon or the Fifteen Fry-up. *On the Beach, Watergate Bay TR8 4AA.* ☎ *01637 861000. www.fifteencornwall.co.uk. Breakfast £4.40–9.30, lunch £14.70–22.55 (3-course set menu £25.45), dinner tasting menu (6 courses) £55. MC, V. Breakfast 8:30–10:30am (last orders 10am); lunch midday–5pm; dinner from 7pm.*

★★ Tregenna House

This former vicarage, dating from the 1860s, now provides spacious and comfortable B&B accommodation in the pretty village of Crantock, a stone's throw from Newquay. It has extensive grounds, with outdoor swimming pool, outdoor seating and a conservatory, and a residents' bar and lounge (with Internet access): light snacks are available midday–9:30pm. The Country Suite on the second floor has its own sitting room and is suitable for families. *West Pentire Road, Crantock TR8 5RZ.* ☎ *01637 830222. www.tregennahouse.co.uk. 5 rooms. MC, V. £32.50–pppn.*

★★ Whipsiderry Hotel

Just north of Newquay overlooking lovely Porth Beach, this family-owned hotel offers comfortable accommodation. Set in more than 2 acres (¾ hectare) of gardens, with an outdoor swimming pool and children's play area, the hotel has a restaurant (six-course dinners), bar lounge and patio area. *Porth TR7 3LY.* ☎ *01637 874777. www.whipsiderry.co.uk. 20 rooms. MC, V. £61–73 dinner/B&B pppn.*

★★ Windswept Café

This new, wooden-built café with a large balcony has a stunning position above Fistral Beach. You can slump on a beanbag or sit on the balcony and soak up the sun. Relaxed, cool ambience plus a great range of dishes from panini to mussels, fish cakes and ostrich steak. Great monthly pudding nights, with the chance to try four different puds after a simple main course. *South Fistral Beach, Esplanade Road TR7 1QA.* ☎ *01637 850793. www.windsweptcafe.co.uk. Mains £9–12. WiFi. MC, V. Mon–Tues 10am–6pm, Wed–Sat 6pm–late.*

Padstow

1 Tourist Information Centre
2 National Lobster Hatchery
3 Padstow Museum
4 St Petroc's Church
5 Prideaux Place
6 Camel Trail
7 Port Isaac
8 Port Quin
9 Saints' Way
10 South West Coast Path
11 Wadebridge

Where to Stay & Dine

Chough Bakery 12

Metropole 13

Pescadou 14

Rick Stein's Café 15

Stein's Fish & Chips 16

Symply Padstow 17

Trevone Beach House 18

ince the mid-1970s, celebrity chef Rick Stein has put the spotlight on the little fishing town of **Padstow**. The narrow streets are often clogged with visitors, and the local fishing fleet struggles to meet the demand for lobster, crabs and crayfish. But there's more to Padstow than trendy eating places: the town has a long and interesting history. Celtic missionary St Petroc founded a monastery here in about A.D. 600. Sir Walter Raleigh lived in the town when he was Warden of Cornwall. During the 17th century, Padstow had a thriving shipbuilding industry, and exported much slate and copper. It was the Cornish terminus of the Southern Railway, which closed in the 1960s.

Padstow harbour.

❶ Tourist Information Centre. Padstow's TIC also serves Wadebridge and the surrounding area; pick up the free street map. *The Red Brick Building, North Quay, Padstow PL28 8AF. ☎ 01841 533449. www. padstowlive.com.*

❷ National Lobster Hatchery. If you want to adopt a lobster, or get involved in marine conservation, pay a visit here. Local fishermen bring in pregnant 'hens' (female lobsters), whose young are reared in captivity before being returned to the sea when large enough to be safe from predators. ⏱ *1 hr. South Quay, Padstow PL28 8BL. ☎ 01841 533877. www.nationallobster*

hatchery.co.uk. Adult £3, child (ages 6–15) £1.50, under-5s free, senior citizen £2, family £7. Daily all year from 10am.

❸ Padstow Museum. This is the place to learn about Padstow's history and traditions, and its much-revered and hard-working lifeboat. One of the town's most colourful festivals is its Hobby Horse cavalcade on May Day (possibly a modern version of a pagan fertility rite), when locals and visitors follow the cavorting 'obby 'oss through the narrow streets to a hypnotic drumbeat. ⏱ *1 hr. The Institute, Market Place PL28 8AL. ☎ 01841 5 32752. www.padstowmuseum.co.uk. Adult*

Padstow sits on the beautiful Camel estuary.

£1, child (under 16) free. Easter–end Oct Mon–Fri 10:30am–4:30pm, Sat 10:30am–1pm.

4 St Petroc's Church. St Petroc, son of a Welsh prince, is said to have spent 30 years in Padstow, and from the 6th to the 9th centuries when it was the religious centre of north Cornwall. The Danes destroyed his original monastery in the year 981; the present church was built between 1425 and 1450. The stump of a Celtic cross lies inside the churchyard's south gate. The church marks the end of the Saints' Way (p 74). ⏱ *30 min. www. padstowparishchurch.co.uk.*

5 Prideaux Place. *See p 59.*

6 Camel Trail. *See p 85.*

Places of Interest Nearby
7 Port Isaac. This quaint old fishing village has seen a huge increase in visitor numbers since providing the picturesque backdrop for a popular TV series. It's a steep walk from the cliff-top car park to the harbour, but don't attempt to drive through the village in high season. On foot, you can explore the 'drangs' (alleys) lined with slate-hung cottages; or climb Roscarrock Hill for the best views. There are lots of eating places, and the catch of the day is on sale at harbour booths on The

Platt (a broad concrete slipway leading to the sea). The former pilchard-fishing hamlet of **8 Port Quin,** 3 miles (4¾km) west, is known as 'the village that died': legend has it that every local man perished in a single disastrous shipwreck in the 19th century. ⏱ *2 hr.*

9 Saints' Way. *See p 74.*

10 South West Coast Path. Take a short ferry trip across the Camel estuary to Rock to follow the South West northeast from Padstow. An easy walk on the west bank leads north of Padstow past Harbour Cove and Hawker's Cove, en route to Stepper Point (p 77).

11 Wadebridge. Around 8 miles (13km) inland lies the town of Wadebridge, at the lowest bridging point of the River Camel. This historic town was granted a market charter in 1313. The 17-arch stone bridge was built in the 15th century. Wadebridge draws the crowds on August bank holidays for the Cornwall Folk Festival. Poetry lovers should visit the John Betjeman Centre in the old railway station on Southern Way (☎ 01208 812392; www.john betjeman.org.uk); recitals of his work are held on summer evenings on Brae Hill, overlooking his grave at St Enodoc church. ⏱ *2 hr. www. visitwadebridge.com.*

Where to **Stay & Dine**

★★ **Chough Bakery**   This award-winning bakery is the place to try a fine Cornish pasty: watch out for seagulls, which may try to steal your alfresco meal. *3 The Strand, Padstow PL28 8AJ. ☎ 01841 532835. www.thechoughbakery. co.uk. Mon–Fri 10am–5pm, Sat 10am–2pm.*

★★ **Metropole**   An imposing but unstuffy Victorian hotel on a hill above the harbour. The best rooms are spacious with excellent views over the town and estuary. The hotel has its own parking and an outdoor swimming pool, open in July and August. *Station Road PL28 8DB. ☎ 0800 2300 365. www.the-metropole.co.uk. 58 rooms. WiFi. MC, V, AmEx. £144–216 per room per night.*

★★ **Pescadou**   The seafood restaurant of the harbour-front Old Custom House Hotel has a well-earned reputation for wonderfully fresh seafood. Open for breakfast, lunch and dinner, it serves dishes such as baked cod over chorizo, sweetcorn and red pepper risotto, and grilled day-boat scallops. *South Quay PL28 8BL. ☎ 01841 532359. www.theold customhouse.co.uk/pescadou.html. Mains £12.95–17.95. MC, V. Daily 10:30am–dinner from 7pm.*

★★★ **Rick Stein's Café**   The most relaxing member of Rick Stein's restaurant portfolio: cushions, wooden floors, white-painted walls and a gentle buzz of conversation. Delicious local fare: Mount's Bay sardines, salt and pepper prawns, mushroom and parmesan omelette, plus roasted vanilla plums with crème fraiche or Treleaven's ice cream. *10 Middle Street PL28 8AP. ☎ 01841 532700. www.rick stein.com. Mains £10.50–16.95. MC, V. Daily 8am–9:30pm (booking recommended in evening).*

★★ **Stein's Fish & Chips**   Eat in (more expensive) or takeaway anything from grilled plaice to battered squid or monkfish, but expect long queues in season. Beef dripping is used for most dishes; a few are cooked in vegetable oil for non-meat eaters. *South Quay PL28 8BL. ☎ 01841 532700. www.rickstein. com. Mains (takeaway) £5–10.75. MC, V. Daily midday–2:30pm, 5–8pm.*

★★ **Symply Padstow**   This elegant, spacious Edwardian house lies in a quiet road a few minutes' walk from the harbour, with lovely views over the Camel estuary. The rooms are exquisitely furnished and decked with fresh flowers. Two self-catering cottages and a bungalow are also available. *32 Dennis Road PL28 8DE. ☎ 01841 532814. www. symply-padstow.co.uk. 4 rooms. WiFi. MC, V. £80–102 per room per night.*

★★★ **Trevone Beach House**   The Padstow area is famed for its wonderful beaches. This stylishly renovated 1930s house is ideal if you want to stay near Padstow but also make the most of the beach. There's a spacious breakfast room and guest lounge, and storage for wetsuits and surfboards; everything is fresh, bright and 'green' wherever possible. *Trevone Bay, Padstow PL28 8QX. ☎ 01841 520469. www.trevone beach.co.uk. 9 rooms. WiFi. MC, V, AmEx. £79–100 per room per night.*

Penzance

1. Tourist Information Centre
2. Chapel Street
3. Penlee House Gallery & Museum
4. Morrab Garden
5. Jubilee Pool
6. Trinity House National Lighthouse Centre
7. Chysauster
8. Marazion
9. Newlyn
10. South West Coast Path
11. St Michael's Mount
12. St Ives Bay Line
13. Wild Bird Hospital & Sanctuary

Where to Stay & Dine
Archie Brown's Health Food Shop & Vegetarian Café 14
Camilla House 15
Honey Pot 16
Navy Inn 17
Olive Farm 18
Penrose Guest House 19
Summer House 20

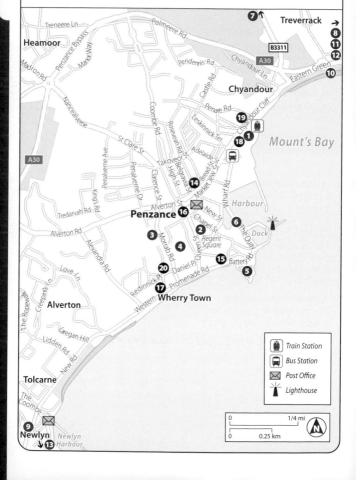

The Cornish name Pen Sans (holy headland) refers to an ancient chapel that once stood on a point west of the harbour. Cornwall's biggest and most westerly town received its first royal charter in 1512 and became an important pilchard-fishing centre, before being destroyed by fire during a Spanish raid in 1595. The export of tin revived the town's fortunes in the 19th century, along with the arrival of the Great Western Railway in 1859. Today, Penzance makes an ideal base for exploring West Penwith.

1 Tourist Information Centre. Ask for the town trail leaflet. The station next door contains a mural of ceramic tiles made by local schoolchildren. *Station Approach TR18 2NF.* ☎ *01736 362207. www. visit-westcornwall.com.*

2 Chapel Street. One of Penzance's most historic streets, this links the Market Place to the harbour. Buildings date largely from the 18th century; look out for the Egyptian House (1835–36) and the Gothic Revival St Mary's Church (1835); also note that no 25 was home to Maria Branwell, mother of the Brontë sisters Charlotte, Emily and Anne. 🕐 *1 hr.*

3 Penlee House Gallery & Museum. *See p 49.*

4 Morrab Garden. These beautiful subtropical gardens, with a bandstand, are surrounded by elegant Regency terraces. Some of the magnolias are 100 years old and the giant echiums (tall purple-blue spires) are a rarity. The Morrab Library in the gardens is one of the UK's few remaining private libraries. 🕐 *30 min–1hr. Closed at dusk.*

5 Jubilee Pool. This huge and splendid tidal bathing pool built into the near Battery Rocks in 1935 is a fine example of Art Deco style. It has sunloungers, deckchairs and a poolside café. 🕐 *2–3 hr. The Promenade.* ☎ *01736 369224. www.jubilee pool.co.uk. Adult £3.30, child (under 12) £2.20, family £12.20. Daily late*

The Egyptian House.

May–Sept 10:30am–6pm (7pm Thurs).

6 Trinity House National Lighthouse Centre. The museum has one of the finest collections of lighthouse equipment in the world, with examples from local sites: Eddystone, Bishop Rock, Longships and Wolf Rock. 🕐 *1½ hr. The Old Buoy Store, Wharf Road TR18 4BN.* ☎ *01736 360077. Daily mid-Mar– end Oct 11am–5pm.*

Places of Interest Nearby
7 Chysauster. *See p 54.*

8 Marazion. *See p 48.*

9 Newlyn. *See p 43.*

St Michael's Mount viewed from Marazion.

⑩ South West Coast Path.
Beyond the busy main road section through Newlyn, the South West west of Penzance makes its way through an idyllic bit of scenery via **Mousehole** (p 43), Lamorna Cove, **Porthcurno** (p 79) and Porthgwarra, before winding round towards Lands End. It is particularly magical in spring, when the cliffs are awash with violets and daffodils.

⑪ St Michael's Mount. *See p 57.*

⑫ St Ives Bay Line. Take the train to St Ives via St Erth (the main railway line connection); you can return by rail or bus, or even walk part of the way (see the TIC town trail leaflet). The line first opened in 1877 and runs past the Hayle Estuary Nature Reserve (RSPB). *🕐 up to 55 min. Traveline 0871 200 2233. www.traveline.org.uk.*

⑬ Wild Bird Hospital & Sanctuary. The hospital, founded in 1928, treats around 1500 sick and injured birds every year and has about 100 permanent residents. *🕐 1 hr. Raginnis Hill, Mousehole TR19 6SR. ☎ 01736 731386. www.mouseholebirdhospital.org.uk. Free admission. Open most days.*

Where to **Stay & Dine**

★★★ Archie Brown's Health Food Shop & Vegetarian Café This is a real find: a health food shop downstairs and café upstairs. Bright, cheerful and relaxed, with a children's play area, newspapers and local photos on the walls. In this long-established, well-regarded café, all is freshly made, largely organic and local: mushroom and hazelnut burger, homity pie and mixed salad, apple and apricot crumble, plus a great range of teas, coffees, smoothies and juices. Blackboards convey the beneficial effects of various herbs and spices.

Bread Street TR18 2EQ. ☎ 01736 362828. www.archiebrowns.co.uk. Mains £4.50–7.50. MC, V. Daily 9am–5pm, plus Sat 7–9pm (booking preferred).

★★★ Camilla House This elegant, grand house on a private road with sea views was built in 1836 for a master mariner. It's now a very stylish B&B (licensed): each room is beautifully decorated, with super views from the top floor. Evening meals are available by arrangement, using fresh local or home-grown produce. The owners know the area well and can suggest local walks or outings (bikes and picnics available on request). *12 Regent Terrace TR18 4DW.* ☎ *01736 363771. www. camillahouse.co.uk. 8 rooms. WiFi. MC, V, AmEx. £75–85 per room per night.*

★★★ **Honey Pot** This cosy eating place with cushioned window seats is located opposite the Acorn Arts Centre. In 1860, the building housed a tobacconist and bar, and has long been a local meeting place. Large portions of delicious homecooked food are available such as lasagne and salad, and sweetcorn fritters, plus a tempting range of cakes and desserts: stem ginger cake, lemon and lime cheesecake, chocolate fridge cake. Picnics can be supplied for evenings at the Minack Theatre (p 35). *5 Parade Street TR18 4 BU.* ☎ *01736 368686. Mains £6.50–8.75. Mon–Sat 10am–6pm, food served midday–5:30pm; plus takeaway.*

★★★ **Navy Inn** This lovely old pub, with bare floorboards and a traditional bar, has a well-deserved reputation for excellent food. All starters can be ordered as main courses including tower of Newlyn crab, fisherman's pie, mixed grill of local fish and spiced sweet potato risotto, plus mouthwatering puddings. Good service and relaxing atmosphere. *Lower Queen Street TR18 4DE.* ☎ *01736 333232. www. navyinn.co.uk. Mains £9.50–18.95. MC, V. Daily midday–2:30pm, 6–9pm.*

★★★ **Olive Farm** A wonderful restaurant in an unlikely situation above a deli opposite the town car park; it's long and narrow with low lighting, a small bar area and an open kitchen. The ambience is relaxed and chatty ambience while generous portions of excellent local food are served: smoked salmon and prawn fishcakes, Tuscan bean stew, wild mushroom and wilted

The Summer House.

spinach risotto, salads, meze and daily specials. Some seats are available outside on the broad pavement. *Wharf Road TR18 2GB.* ☎ *01736 359009. Mains £6.50–12.95. MC, V, AmEx. Wed–Mon 10am–9:30pm, Tues lunchtime only.*

★ **Penrose Guest House** This small, comfortable, handy B&B on a quiet road near the station is a Grade II listed Georgian town house, around 200 years old, with many original features and a lovely southfacing mature garden. *8 Penrose Terrace TR18 4HQ.* ☎ *01736 362782. www.penrosegsthse.co.uk. 3 rooms. MC, V. £52–78 per room per night.*

★★★ **Summer House** A touch of the Mediterranean in a quiet street close to the sea with frescoes, potted palms and breakfast in the garden. This elegantly refurbished former dower house dates from 1791. Every room is different and beautifully designed in seaside colours; some have double-aspect views. Gourmet four-course dinners are served at weekends. *Cornwall Terrace TR18 4HL.* ☎ *01736 363744. www.summerhouse-cornwall.com. 5 rooms. WiFi. MC, V. £95–125 per room per night.*

St Ives

1 Tourist Information Centre
2 Tate St Ives
3 Barbara Hepworth Museum
   & Sculpture Gallery
4 The Island & St Nicholas Chapel
5 The Sloop Craft Market
6 St Ives Museum
7 Church of St Ia
8 Paradise Park
9 St Ives Bay Line

10 South West Coast Path
11 Zennor

Where to Stay & Dine

Cornerways Bed & Breakfast Guest House 12
Dolphin Fish & Chips 13
The Nook 14
Olives 15
Onshore 16
Porthminster Hotel 17
The Union Inn 18

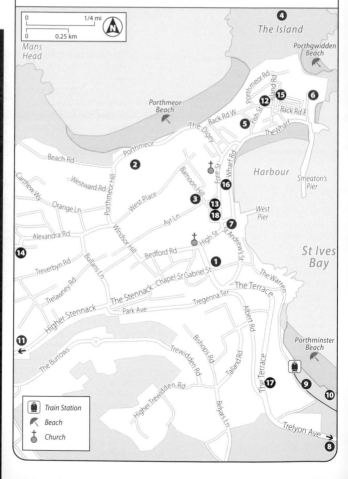

The old fishing port of St Ives has attracted artists and holidaymakers since the late 19th century for the beauty of its coastline and the quality of the light. The arrival of the railway in 1877 was a great boost to the town. Despite the crowds thronging the narrow streets of Downlong (the oldest part, around the harbour) during the holiday season, it remains a charming place. In 1939, the artistic duo Barbara Hepworth (1903–75) and Ben Nicholson (1901–30) moved to St Ives, creating a dynamic and influential artists' enclave that lasts to this day (p 46).

❶ Tourist Information Centre.
The Guildhall, Street an Pol TR26 2DS. ☎ *01736 796297. www.visit-westcornwall.com.*

❷ Tate St Ives and **❸ Barbara Hepworth Museum & Sculpture Gallery.** The spectacular Tate St Ives art gallery with its swirling spiral forms makes a dramatic seafront statement. Designed and built by Eldred Evans and David Shalev, it opened in June 1993, focusing mainly on works by local artists from the 1880s to the present day. It also hosts travelling exhibitions, workshops and courses. The huge stained-glass window at the entrance is by the renowned Cornish artist Patrick Heron. The Barbara Hepworth Museum is a stone's throw away (p 47). 🕐 *4 hr. Porthmeor Beach TR26 1TG.* ☎ *01736 796226.*

The Tate St Ives, seen from The Island.

www.tatestives.co.uk. Daily Mar–Oct 10am–5pm; Nov–Feb Tue–Sun 10am–4pm. Tate St Ives: adult £5.75, child (18 and under) free, concessions £3.25; Barbara Hepworth Museum: adult £4.75, child (18 and under) free, concessions £2.75, joint admission adult £8.75, concessions £4.50.

❹ The Island & St Nicholas Chapel. The Island is a local name for St Ives' Head, a grassy promontory between the harbour and Porthmeor Beach. The traditional seamen's chapel on the Island serves as a seamark, and has splendid bay views. 🕐 *20 min to walk there and back.*

❺ The Sloop Craft Market. Tucked behind the Sloop Inn, this delightful market in medieval fish cellars consists of interesting craft

St Nicholas Chapel.

workshops. ⏱ *15–30 min.* ☎ *01736 796584.*

6 St Ives Museum. Housed in an old seaman's mission on the Island, this eclectic museum covers many weird and wonderful aspects of St Ives' history; follow the signs from Smeaton's Pier on the harbour. ⏱ *1½ hr. Wheal Dream TR26 1PR.* ☎ *01736 796005. Free admission. Easter–Oct Mon–Fri 10am–5pm, Sat 10am–4pm.*

7 Church of St Ia. The mid-15th century parish church is dedicated to an Irish priestess who brought Christianity to this part of Cornwall in the 5th century, and is said to have crossed the Irish Sea on a leaf. St Ia's holy well is near the Tate St Ives, overlooking Porthmeor Beach; until 1843 it was the main water

supply for Downlong. ⏱ *30 min. St Andrews Street.*

Places of Interest Nearby
8 Paradise Park. *See p 36.*

9 St Ives Bay Line. *See p 130.*

10 South West Coast Path. One of the most stunning stretches of the South West leads to Lands End.

11 Zennor is the first place you reach after a tough 5 miles (8km) walk, famous for the Tinners' Arms, the Wayside Museum (p 54) and the legend of the Zennor mermaid, who lured a local fisherman to her watery home; his voice can still be heard beneath waves. A mermaid is carved on a pew end in St Senara's church. ⏱ *30 min.*

Where to **Stay & Dine**

★★★ Cornerways Bed & Breakfast Guest House

Treat yourself to a night or two at this delightful guesthouse just off Island Square. Daphne du Maurier (p 107) stayed here in the 1940s; the quirky rooms are named after characters from her books. All are en suite and two have lovely sea views across the rooftops (although upper rooms involve narrow stairways). Breakfast includes wonderful homemade preserves. *1 Bethesda Place TR26 1PA.* ☎ *01736 796706. www.cornerways stives.com. 6 rooms. WiFi. MC, V. £60–90 per room per night.*

★★ Dolphin Fish & Chips

Look no further for good, reasonably priced local fish and chips. You can bring your own beer or wine to this bright, cheerful, licensed establishment, and sit upstairs enjoying harbour views (meals arrive via a dumb waiter): flowers on tables and excellent service. *Fore Street TR26 1HE.* ☎ *01736 795701. Mains ca. £5.35; specials such as two meals for £7.50. Daily 11am–7pm; to ca. 10pm in summer.*

★ The Nook

This recently renovated house in the upper town has clean, comfortable, modern rooms and off-street parking, which compensate for the lack of sea views or old-town charm. Good breakfast and large residents' lounge. *Ayr TR26 1EQ.* ☎ *01736 795913. www.the nookstives.co.uk. 16 rooms, incl. 2 singles. WiFi. MC, V. £37.50–49 pppn.*

★★★ Olives

Steps lead up to this little sunflower-filled café-restaurant with a continental feel, which is a gem in the oldest and most atmospheric part of town. Huge cakes and desserts are on show, such as treacle and orange pecan tart, Dutch apple cake, fruit pavlova, as well as chunky vegetable soup, caramelised onion and vintage cheddar quiche and an evening special dish (bring your own alcohol). Everything is homemade in the tiny kitchen, and all ingredients sourced locally (meat is organic where possible). *Island Square TR26 1AB.* ☎ *07873 750977. Mains around £5.95. Summer 10am–6pm, 7–10pm, winter midday–5/6pm plus Fri & Sat eves.*

★ Onshore

One of the best harbour-front choices, Onshore is bright, sleek and modern, with an open kitchen and traditional pizza oven. Local mussels, St Ives bay mackerel, seafood risotto plus a good range of salads, pasta, tapas, breads and dips are available, as well as a daily specials board, Fair Trade and local produce. *Wharf Road TR26 1LF.* ☎ *01736 796000. Mains £6.95– 12.95. MC, V. Daily 9am–3pm, 6pm– 9pm (longer hours in summer).*

★★ Porthminster Hotel

An elegant, spacious hotel overlooking Porthminster Beach and subtropical gardens. It has a range of luxury suites (one with double spa bath), and family rooms; amenities include a restaurant, leisure centre, tennis courts, and indoor and outdoor swimming pools. *The Terrace TR26 2BN,* ☎ *01736 795221. www.porthminster-hotel.co.uk. 42 rooms. WiFi. MC, V. £60–150 pppn dinner, B&B.*

★ The Union Inn

This unpretentious local pub makes a welcome relief from the trendier harbourside establishments. Interesting old photographs on the walls portray St Ives' fishermen in past times. Excellent reasonably priced fisherman's pie, local sole, mackerel fillets, cauliflower cheese and Sunday lunches. *Fore Street TR26 1HE.* ☎ *01736 796486. Mains £5.95–9.95. MC, V. Daily 11am–1am.*

Truro

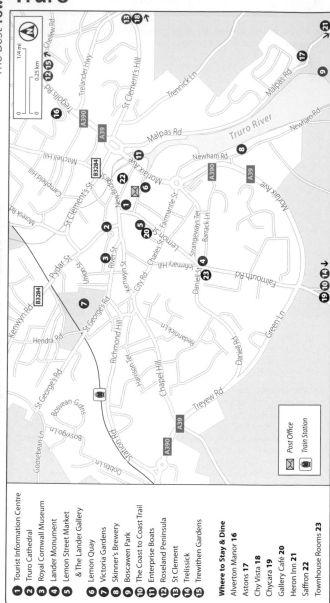

0   1/4 mi
0   0.25 km

1 Tourist Information Centre
2 Truro Cathedral
3 Royal Cornwall Museum
4 Lander Monument
5 Lemon Street Market
   & The Lander Gallery
6 Lemon Quay
7 Victoria Gardens
8 Skinner's Brewery
9 Boscawen Park
10 The Coast to Coast Trail
11 Enterprise Boats
12 Roseland Peninsula
13 St Clement
14 Trelissick
15 Trewithen Gardens

Where to Stay & Dine
Alverton Manor 16
Astons 17
Chy Vista 18
Chycara 19
Gallery Café 20
Heron Inn 21
Saffron 22
Townhouse Rooms 23

Post Office
Train Station

Cornwall's county town lies at the meeting place of three rivers: Truro, Kenwyn and Allen. Although not the county's largest urban settlement, Truro is the main shopping centre. An enviable heritage of Georgian, Regency and Victorian buildings in the largely pedestrianised town centre, and its imposing cathedral, lend it status. Around 800 years ago Truro was a market town and tin-exporting port; today pleasure cruisers, not merchant ships, make the journey downriver towards Falmouth.

❶ Tourist Information Centre.
The TIC is located under the town clock, near the Hall for Cornwall, the county's leading entertainment centre. *Municipal Buildings, Boscawen Street TR1 2NE.* ☎ *01872 263031. www.truro.gov.uk. Hall for Cornwall:* ☎ *01872 262466. www.hallfor cornwall.co.uk.*

❷ Truro Cathedral. The Gothic-style cathedral, with its impressive 250ft (76m) tower and green spire, was built between1880 and 1910, replacing the medieval church of St Mary's that previously stood here (a surviving remnant now forms the south aisle). The cathedral's Victorian stained glass is remarkable. 🕑 *1 hr. St Marys Street.* ☎ *01872 276782. www.trurocathedral.org.uk. Mon–Sat 7:30 am–6pm (from 9:30am Bank Hols), Sun 9am–7pm. Donations greatly received.*

Truro Cathedral.

Lander Monument.

❸ Royal Cornwall Museum.
The oldest and largest museum in the county was founded in 1818 for 'the promotion of knowledge in natural history, ethnology and the fine and industrial arts, especially in relation to Cornwall'. Unsurprisingly, it has an impressive geology section. 🕑 *2 hr. River Street.* ☎ *01872 272205. www.royalcornwallmuseum. org.uk. Admission free. Mon–Sat 10am–4:45pm (closed Bank Hols).*

❹ Lander Monument. This lofty column was erected in 1835 to commemorate the explorer brothers Richard and John Lander, intrepid local heroes who discovered the source of the Nile. *Top of Lemon Street.*

❺ Lemon Street (permanent) Market & The Lander Gallery. Lemon Street market is a great little area of individual shops and Classic Cornish art at the Lander Gallery. *www.lemonstreetmarket.co.uk.*

❻ Lemon Quay. A lively space of shops and eating places in the centre of Truro, near the bus station, Hall for Cornwall (where there's a weekly flea market) and Pannier Market; farmers' markets Wed and Sat, country market Tues, and specialist markets throughout the year. ⏱ *1–2 hr. Lemon Quay.*

❼ Victoria Gardens. A well-maintained public park, created to celebrate Queen Victoria's Jubilee, with a bandstand and fountain; the majestic granite viaduct (1904) carries the mainline Paddington–Penzance railway, Isambard Kingdom Brunel's original version (1859). Brass band concerts are held on Sunday afternoons (end May–end Sept). ⏱ *30 min–1hr. St George's Road.*

❽ Skinner's Brewery. This brewery, which holds tastings and tours and has a shop, is the producer of Betty Stogs, winner of the Champion Best Bitter of Great Britain Award 2008, and award-winning Cornish Knocker. All ales, lagers and ciders are named after characters in Cornish folklore. ⏱ *2 hr. Riverside, Newham TR1 2DP.* ☎ *01872 245689. www.skinnersbrewwery. com. Tours: Easter–Oct Mon–Fri midday & 2:30pm.*

❾ Boscawen Park. Named after the distinguished Cornishman Admiral Edward Boscawen (1711–61), and built on an old landfill site, these beautiful gardens by the Truro river also contain Truro's Cricket Club, tennis courts and football pitches. ⏱ *30 min–1hr. Malpas Road.*

A riot of summer colour in Boscawen Park.

Places of Interest Nearby
❿ The Coast to Coast Trail. A cross-Cornwall cycle route; p 87.

⓫ Enterprise Boats. The only boat service linking Truro and Falmouth, from Truro (high tide) or Malpas (low tide); trips to Trelissick Gardens (p 28). ⏱ *1 hr from Falmouth to Truro and also 1 hr from Falmouth to Malpas. Town Quay.* ☎ *01326 374241. www.enterprise-boats.co.uk.*

⓬ Roseland Peninsula. *See p 155.*

⓭ St Clement. A couple of miles southeast of Truro on the Tresillian river, St Clement is a pretty little hamlet with a 15th-century church and an artist's workshop (Lychgate Studio). Gentle walks lead upriver to Tresillian (more scenic at high tide); an inland path leads to Malpas. ⏱ *30 min.*

⓮ Trelissick. *See p 28.*

⓯ Trewithen Gardens. *See p 28.*

Where to **Stay & Dine**

★★★ **Alverton Manor**   This impressive Grade II listed building stands in extensive grounds just minutes from the city centre. It has mullioned windows, a fine slate roof and a real sense of history and it has been restored to its former grandeur. *Tregolls Road TR1 1ZQ.* ☎ *01872 276633. www.alvertonmanor.co.uk. 33 rooms. WiFi (in lounge bar). MC, V. £140–205 per room per night.*

★★★ **Astons**   This attractive bar-restaurant in Boscawen Park enjoys a lovely setting, with easy parking and terrace dining in fine weather. The interior has been completely refurbished: wood floors, lime and cerise colour schemes, local artwork and an ingenious partially glazed extension. The food reflects the cool, stylish ambience: Cornish halibut with citrus braised fennel, risotto of sweet potato and coriander, Cornish crab and herb linguine. Takeaway is available. *Malpas Road TR1 1SG.* ☎ *01872 2721121. www. astonstrutro.com. Mains £9.95– 12.95. MC, V. Daily 11am–ca. 11pm.*

★★ **Chy Vista**   Only a mile (1½km) from the centre of Truro, and yet completely secluded in beautiful countryside, Chy Vista is one of a group of tastefully converted farm buildings (formerly a barn) standing in its own immaculate walled garden: excellent breakfasts. *Higher Penair, St Clement TR1 1TD.* ☎ *01872 270592. 2 rooms. Open Mar–Oct. £58–62 per room per night. No credit cards.*

★★★ **Chycara**   A rural find just a 10–15 minutes drive from Truro. Great for families, in 16 acres (6½ hectares) of landscaped gardens, with an indoor swimming pool, fitness equipment, Jacuzzi and tennis court, and easy access to the Coast-to-Coast cycle trail at Bissoe; it's also on National Cycle Route 2, a day's ride from Penzance. The two- or three-bedroom lodges are completely private. Single-night bookings accepted. *Chyreen Lane, Carnon Downs TR3 6LG.* ☎ *01872 865447. www.chycara.co.uk. 5 rooms, 2 lodges. WiFi (in rooms). MC, V. £65*

River views from the Heron Inn.

Heron Inn at Malpas.

per room per night; single from £45; reduction for more than 3 nights. Lodges £70–135 per night.

★★★ **Gallery Café** Part of the Lander Gallery on the upper floor of Lemon Street Market, Cornish foods are a speciality here: Tregothnan teas, Helford Creek apple juice, stuffed Tregonning mushrooms, beef, Betty Stogs ale and chestnut stew, as well as tapas, open toasties, salads and tempting muffins and cakes. A lovely place to chill out, surrounded by a wide range of Cornish fine art spanning four centuries. *Lemon Street Market, Lemon Street TR1 2PN.* ☎ *01872 275578. www.landergallery.co.uk. Mains £6.75–7.25. MC, V. Mon–Sat 9am–5:30pm; breakfast to 11am, lunch 11:30am–3pm.*

★★ **Heron Inn** Malpas is a pretty village near the meeting point of the Truro and Tresillian rivers, with lovely views (parking can be tricky). In a lovely riverside setting, the Heron Inn has plenty of seating inside and out and serves reasonably priced traditional pub food: lasagne with garlic bread, spicy crab cakes, fish and chips, tortilla wraps and panini. All food is cooked to order. *Trenhale Terrace, Malpas TR1 1SQ.* ☎ *01872 272773. www.heroninn.co.uk. Mains £5.25–7.95. MC, V. Daily 11am–11pm.*

★★★ **Saffron** Home-cooked locally sourced ingredients make this place a gastronomic delight. Saffron uses seasonal produce: in early summer asparagus, in midsummer blackcurrants, raspberries, globe artichokes, broad beans . . . all grown on nearby farms. The inventive menu includes such temptations as panfried scallops with rhubarb butter sauce, stove-seared hake and the Tregassow asparagus plate: soupcon, fritter, steamed, grilled, seared and risotto! Look out for the 'Cornish Ten Deadly Sins' brunch. *5 Quay Street TR1 2HB.* ☎ *01872 263771. www.saffronrestauranttruro.co.uk. Mains £12–16. £19.50 for 3 courses. MC, V. Summer kitchen menu from 5pm. Summer 10am–10pm; call for winter opening.*

★ **Townhouse Rooms** Simple, convenient B&B just a 5-minute walk from the city centre. It serves continental buffet breakfast, and tea, cakes and snacks are available all day; you can bring back a takeaway and a bottle of wine if you like. There's also a laundry service, drying room, bike lock-up and off-road parking. *20 Falmouth Road TR1 2HX.* ☎ *01872 277374. www.trurotownhouse.com. 12 rooms. WiFi. MC, V. £79 per room per night.* ●

Bodmin Moor **& the North Coast**

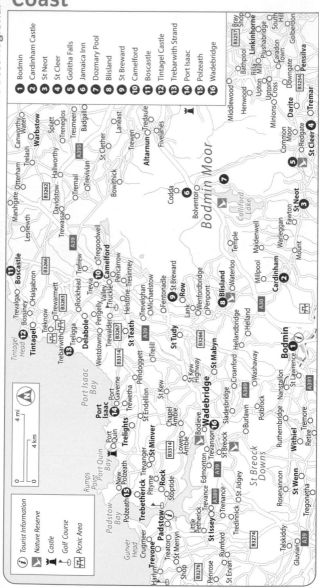

Previous page: Lighthouse and the Big Pool, St Agnes.

The A30 climbs over Bodmin Moor soon after crossing the Devon–Cornwall border at the Tamar river. By sticking to the main road, as most travellers do, you miss many of Cornwall's best-kept secrets. Tucked away down single-track lanes and wooded valleys lie splendid villages, churches and prehistoric monuments, often shrouded in age-old legends. Tracking them down, of course, can be tricky. For a complete contrast to the lonely uplands northeast of Bodmin, this tour continues along one of the most scenic sections of the north coast: via rugged cliffs, fishing villages, surfing beaches and the evocative ruins of Tintagel Castle. **START: Bodmin. Trip Distance: 87 miles (140km). Trip Length: 2 days. Maps: OS Explorers 106, 109, 111.**

1 Bodmin. *See p 93.*

Follow the signs to the A38 Liskeard. Cross the A30; turn left to Cardinham. Pick up signs to the Mount. Note the left turn (dead-end) to Cardinham Castle. Distance: 5 miles (8km).

2 Cardinham Castle. Little remains of the early stone castle at Cardinham, built soon after the Norman Conquest (around 1080) by the Sheriff of Cornwall; the castle is thought to have been in ruins by the 1500s. Look out for the remains of earthworks in a field (no public right of way). 🕐 *15 min. Free admission. Open all year round.*

Continue to Treslea Downs; turn right signposted Mount. Keep ahead to reach St Neot. Distance: 3¾ miles (6km).

3 St Neot. This handsome village nestles in a sheltered valley on the southern edge of the moor; the surrounding parish is the second largest in the county. The name St Neot is thought to be a scrambled version of the 9th-century Celtic saint Anietus. The church of St Anietus dates from the 15th century and contains some superb medieval stained glass. At the top of the tower is an oak branch, replaced every year on Oak Apple Day (29 May): a reminder of

Bodmin Moor signpost.

the village's support for the Royalist cause during the Civil War. The historic London Inn, an old coaching stop, is a popular local landmark by the church. St Neot's holy well lies in water-meadows near the river, where the saint caught his daily quota of just one fish from a miraculous never-ending supply. 🕐 *30 min.*

Just past the church, bear left, signed to St Cleer. Cross the River Fowey on Treverbyn Bridge; turn left on the B3254. Reach King Doniert's Stone on the left (p 55). Turn right for St Cleer. Distance: 6¼ miles (10km).

St Cleer parish church.

4 St Cleer. This solid stone-built village has a 15th-century church and a holy well dedicated to St Clarus, said to be a cure for insanity and blindness. Several non-conformist chapels date from the mid-19th century when miners and their families flooded into the area: the population rose from 982 in 1831 to 3931 in 1861. The Liskeard and Caradon railway line ran along the edge of the graveyard en route to the mining areas on Caradon Hill (p 19). Prehistoric monuments abound in this area, such as King Doniert's Stone (p 55) and Trethevy Quoit (p 55). ⏱ *30 min.*

Retrace your route out of St Cleer; turn left. At Redgate, turn right signposted Bolventor. Pass the sign to Golitha Falls on the left. Distance: 2 miles (3¼km).

Close up of King Doniert's stone.

5 Golitha Falls. Bodmin Moor's best-known beauty spot is a white-water stretch of the River Fowey as it leaves the underlying granite and cascades over softer rocks. Golitha means 'obstruction', a reference to a large boulder that used to block the river. It was blown apart in the 19th century. Look out for two large wheelpits by the river (remains of Wheal Victoria, a brief copper-mining venture). The falls run for about 800 yards (730m). The woodland paths from the large car park (toilets) can be muddy after rain. ⏱ *1 hr. www.golithafalls.co.uk. Free admission. Open all year round.*

Continue to Bolventor. Distance: 6¾ miles (11km).

6 Jamaica Inn. Jamaica Inn was originally a coaching inn, built in 1750 on the turnpike route between Launceson and Bodmin. It was also a notorious hotbed of smuggling (vast quantities of contraband, especially rum and brandy, were illegally imported into the UK via the coasts of Devon and Cornwall). Immortalised in one of Daphne du Maurier's most famous novels, this much-commercialised inn is now an essential stop-off for many visitors traversing Bodmin Moor. The story behind Jamaica Inn (p 107) is told in the small on-site museum (admission fee), which contains a display of smuggling memorabilia. ⏱ *1 hr. Jamaica Inn, Bolventor PL15 7TS. ☎ 01566 86250. www.jamaicainn.co.uk. Daily from 8am for breakfast, last food orders 9pm. Pub open 11am–11pm.*

Join the A30, signed to Bodmin. Pass Colliford Lake Park (left). Turn right, signed Blisland, after 6 miles (9½km). At the crossroads, turn right to village. Distance: 8¾ miles (14km).

Dozmary Pool

Bodmin Moor is full of myths and legends. Opposite Jamaica Inn a lane leads to **7** **Dozmary Pool,** said to be the spot where Sir Bedivere returned King Arthur's sword Excalibur to the Lady of

the Lake after Arthur's death. Its Arthurian links (popularised in early 20th-century guidebooks) are, to say the least, tenuous. Another story claims that the pool is bottomless, but it's actually quite shallow and occasionally dries up in summer. The pool can be viewed only from the road.

Dozmary Pool, place of legends.

8 **Blisland.** This exceptionally pretty village is one of the few in Cornwall with a village green. Its parish church is also unusual—the only one in England dedicated to St Protus (known locally as St Pratt) and St Hyacinth, two brothers martyred in the 3rd century. It has a wonderful interior with a vividly coloured 19th-century rood screen. It dates back to Norman times, when the ancient manor of Blisland was ruled over by King Harold, who died at the Battle of Hastings in 1066. Look out for the medieval manor house and the Blisland Inn (p 95) on the village green, and the Old School (1842) near the church. ⏱ *30 min.*

At the edge of the village green, turn right signposted to St Breward. Bear right at the top corner, signed village hall. Turn left; go straight on at the next junction and then right to Churchtown. Distance: 3½ miles (5½km).

9 **St Breward.** A strung-out settlement on the northeast edge of the moor. Its church is the highest (in altitude) in Cornwall (both the church and the Old Inn are in the northern extension, Churchtown). St Breward prospered on granite quarrying. A holy well in the valley below is dedicated to Branwalader, the original name for St Breward; the waters are said to cure itchy eyes. Our route crosses Garn Bridge, which is a replacement for the original, destroyed by floods in 1847. ⏱ *30 min.*

The Old School, Blisland.

The Blisland Inn.

Pass the church, signed to Camelford. Turn left to Garn Bridge; turn right, and then right again onto the B3266. Meet the A39 at Valley Truckle and turn right to Camelford. Distance: 6 miles (9½km).

⑩ Camelford. Bodmin Moor's highest point, Brown Willy (1375ft/420m), lies not far southeast of Camelford, which at 700ft (214m) above sea level is said to be one of the highest towns in England. This old market town (granted a royal charter in 1259) was once a strategic crossing point of the River Camel. Camelford still suffers from being a through route, and the centre is often clogged with traffic. But peaceful paths lead just off the main street along the banks of the river. Look out for the golden camel weather vane on the town hall. The town's name has nothing to do with camels, however, but is thought to derive from 'Camalanford' (cam means crooked and alan means beautiful). Peck'ish in Victoria Road serves good fish and chips. 🕐 *15 min.*

Retrace the A39 towards Bodmin; turn right onto the B3266 signed Boscastle. Note the Bicycle Museum at Camelford Station (on the right). Descend to Boscastle; turn right for the centre. Distance: 7½ miles (12km).

⑪ Boscastle. This seductive little coastal village hit the headlines in August 2004, when it was devastated by flash floods after exceptionally heavy rain. Buildings and cars were dramatically washed into the sea, but miraculously no lives were lost. The damage was swiftly repaired, leaving few signs of the disaster, and Boscastle retained its popularity with visitors. The village takes its name from an 11th-century castle. It developed first as a fishing port and then as a tourist destination in Victorian times. It has a good range of shops, cafés and pubs. It's worth taking a walk from the village centre along the tortuous riverbank to the harbour, which is protected from the open sea by high cliffs. To your left you can see the site of an Iron Age cliff castle. 🕐 *2 hr.*

Turn left from the car park; pick up the B3263 southwest towards Tintagel. Distance: 3½ miles (5½km).

⑫ Tintagel Castle. *See p 64.*

Boats at Boscastle.

From Tintagel centre, retrace your route to the mini-roundabout and turn right, signed Trebarwith. Pass through Trewarmett; turn right for Trebarwith Strand. Distance: 3½ miles (5½km).

Port Isaac from the Platt.

13 Trebarwith Strand. Worth a visit for a quick walk on the beach (which is accessible only over the rocks at low tide) and a drink at the Port William Inn. ⏰ *30 min.*

Retrace your route to the road junction and turn right. On meeting the B3314 turn right, signed Delabole. Pass through Delabole (famous for the production of Delabole slate); turn left, signposted Port Gaverne. Reach the Port Isaac car park. Distance: 10½ miles (17km).

14 Port Isaac. See p 126.

Follow the B3267 out of Port Isaac. Turn right on the B3314, signed to Wadebridge, and then right signposted Polzeath. Distance: 7¼ miles (11¾km).

15 Polzeath. One of the biggest and best beaches on the north Cornish coast. Understandably it's popular, and a magnet for surfers. A favourite haunt of Sir John Betjeman (p 126), Polzeath has now been taken over by the surfing craze. It has a good range of surf shops and beach cafés, and a huge cliff-top car park. ⏰ *30 min.*

Continue through Trebetherick; at the junction turn left, signed to Wadebridge. Turn right onto the B3314. Turn right for Wadebridge town centre. Distance: 1¾ miles (2¾km).

16 Wadebridge. See p 126.

Retrace your route over the bridge; turn right, signed to Bodmin; rejoin the A389 and turn right. Note the Camel Valley Vineyard right at Washaway (p 94). Follow the route to Bodmin; turn left for the town centre. Distance: 11½ miles (18½km).

Cornwall's **Forgotten Corner**

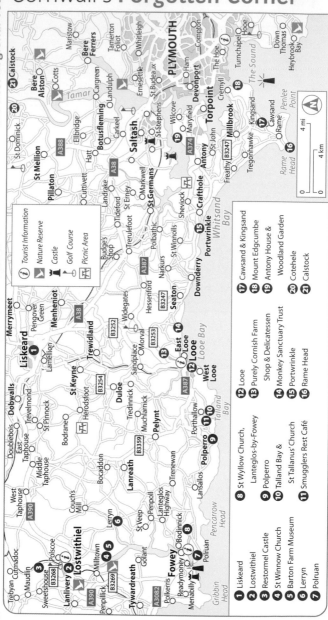

Legend:
- ⓘ Tourist Information
- ⚑ Nature Reserve
- ♜ Castle
- ⛳ Golf Course
- 🏕 Picnic Area

1 Liskeard
2 Lostwithiel
3 Restormel Castle
4 St Winnow Church
5 Barton Farm Museum
6 Lerryn
7 Polruan

8 St Wyllow Church, Lanteglos-by-Fowey
9 Polperro
10 Talland Bay & St Tallanus' Church
11 Smugglers Rest Café

12 Looe
13 Purely Cornish Farm Shop & Delicatessen
14 Monkey Sanctuary Trust
15 Portwrinkle
16 Rame Head

17 Cawsand & Kingsand
18 Mount Edgcumbe
19 Antony House & Woodland Garden
20 Cotehele
21 Calstock

This romantic name applies to the region between the River Tamar (the county boundary with Devon) to the east and the River Fowey to the west. Cornwall's southeast corner is often unfairly bypassed by holidaymakers heading for the sand and surf of the far west, even though it includes popular honeypot villages such as Looe and Polperro. But this relatively quiet area deserves investigation for its historic towns, fishing villages, wooded creeks, ancient churches and sheltered beaches. **START: Liskeard. Trip Distance: 98½ miles (158½km). Trip Length: 4 days. Maps: OS Explorers 107, 108.**

❶ Liskeard. An unexpectedly rewarding town. *See p 114.*

Follow the signs for the A38 via A390 (Looe). Take the A38 to Bodmin. After 5½ (8¾km), at the Twelvewoods roundabout bear left signed to St Austell on the A390. Distance: 13¾ miles (22¼km).

❷ Lostwithiel and **❸ Restormel Castle.** *See p 117 and 61.*

Turn left from the town car park; turn left down Fore Street (just before traffic lights). Cross river; travel uphill and turn right immediately after Earl of Chatham pub. After 2 miles (3¼km) turn right, signed to St Winnow. Distance: 3 miles (4¾km).

❹ St Winnow Church &
❺ Barton Farm Museum. A narrow lane leads to the River Fowey. St Winnow is said to have came to this

peaceful spot in the year 670. His oratory was replaced by a stone building in the 12th century; this was extended in the 15th century and renovated in Victorian times. St Winnow's window depicts him carrying his customary emblematic handmill.
Barton Farm Museum was founded by James Henry Stephens in 1976; his family has farmed here since 1909. It's charmingly informal and contains old farming tools and machinery, and in summer you can get refreshments from a simple kiosk. ⏲ *45 min. St Winnow Barton Farm Museum, St Winnow, Lostwithiel.* ☎ *01208 873742. Free admission. Daily Easter or 1 Apr–end Oct midday–6pm.*

Retrace your route up the lane, bearing right at fork; at T-junction turn right. Distance: 2¾ miles (4½km).

Restormel Castle.

6 Lerryn. A pretty village on a creek, crossed by stepping-stones; 'Lerryn' derives from the Cornish *lerrion*, meaning 'waters'. When Lostwithiel was the principal port on the River Fowey (p 105), supplies were still shipped inland up to Lerryn's quays. The last cargo of limestone (used as a soil conditioner) was offloaded in 1918. The 16th-century Ship Inn is worth a visit. ⏱ *30 min.*

From the car park, turn right; pick up the signs for Polruan. After 3½ (5½km) at Lenteglos Highway, turn right (for Bodinnick Ferry keep straight on); soon turn left for Polruan. Distance: 7¼ miles (11¾km).

7 Polruan. Surrounded on three sides by water, and far less accessible than Fowey (p 105), Polruan is much quieter. It's not suitable for the elderly or infirm because the hill leading up from the harbour (Fore Street—a 1:6 gradient) is extremely steep. Visit the 15th-century blockhouse, once linked by a chain ferry to its opposite number in Fowey. Fishing, smuggling and boatbuilding have kept Polruan afloat for centuries; one last working boatyard survives. ⏱ *2 hr.*

St Winnow Barton Farm Museum.

Travel Tip

If you want to have a look at Fowey, leave your car in Polruan and catch the passenger ferry, or use the Bodinnick car ferry.

Retrace your route out of Polruan; after ½ mile (¾km) turn left, signposted Lanteglos, and then bear right off lane as signed. Distance: 1¼ miles (2km).

8 St Wyllow Church, Lanteglos-by-Fowey. Daphne du Maurier (p 107) was married in this beautiful church in July 1932. The church featured as Lantoc in her first novel, *The Loving Spirit*. Dedicated to a Celtic saint, most of the building dates from the 14th century. Parts of the tower and font are Norman. ⏱ *20 min.*

Continue past the church; turn left at the T-junction. After 1 mile (1½km) bear right onto a single-track lane. At the junction, turn right; at the next junction turn right signed to Polperro; soon afterwards, turn left as signed and descend to Crumplehorn and Polperro car park. Distance: 5 miles (8km).

9 Polperro. Best visited out of high season, this 13th-century fishing village is immensely popular. From the vast car park on the A387 at Crumplehorn walk or take the 'Horse Bus' into the village. The harbour (1300) is delightful; most buildings date from the 16th and 17th centuries. Fishermen's cottages of this period were designed with storage space at street level and living rooms upstairs. During the Napoleonic wars with France, smuggling reached its height; tea, gin and tobacco were brought from the Channel Islands. **Polperro's Model Village** shows how the village looked before the tourist boom. ⏱ *20 min. Polperro's Model Village: Easter–Oct from 10am.*

From the car park, turn sharp left onto the A387. After 1¾ miles (2¾km), turn left on a single-track lane signed to Talland. Distance: 2¾ miles (4½km).

⑩ Talland Bay & St Tallanus' Church. The church is dedicated to the 5th-century hermit St Tallanus, and has an unusual detached bell tower, in an abnormal position to the nave. Don't miss ⑪ the **Smugglers Rest Café** (car park).

Continue along the lane to pass the church. Turn right onto the A387 (to Looe). At West Looe, turn left for the car park. Distance: 3¼ miles (5¼km).

⑫ Looe. *See p 113.*

From the car park, turn left and cross the bridge on the A387; pass the station and turn right onto the B3253 towards Torpoint/Plymouth to reach St Martin. Distance: 1½ miles (2½km).

⑬ Purely Cornish Farm Shop & Delicatessen. The Courtyard Café provides a comfortable break with sofas, newspapers and local literature; light snacks include local sardines or cheese on toast, clotted

Purely Cornish farm shop.

cream teas and so on. The Farm Shop sells high-quality produce from all over Cornwall; make up your own hamper on the spot. *Purely Cornish Farm Shop & Delicatessen, St Martin by Looe, PL13 1NX. ☎ 01503 262680. www.purelycornish.co.uk. Summer daily 10am–5pm (Sun from 11am), winter 10am–4pm (closed Tues/Wed afternoons). Also a delicatessen in East Looe (p 113).*

Turn right onto the B3253. After just over 1 mile (1½km), turn right on a single-track lane at No Man's

Polruan.

Polperro model village.

Land and follow the brown signs for Monkey Sanctuary. Distance: 3 miles (4¾km).

⑭ Monkey Sanctuary Trust.

This environmental charity was set up in 1964 in the grounds of a clifftop Victorian house to protect the threatened Amazonian woolly monkey. The Trust has a breeding colony, runs a rehabilitation scheme for ex-pet monkeys and supports conservation projects and primate rescue centres in South America. ⏱ *3 hr. The Monkey Sanctuary, St Martins, Looe PL13 1NZ.* ☎ *01503 262532. www.monkeysanctuary.org. Adult £7.50, child (ages 5–16) £3.50, family £20, concessions £5. Early Apr– end Sept Sun–Thurs 11am–4:30pm.*

Turn right and keep ahead on the single-track lane signposted Seaton. At the next junction, turn right; in Seaton turn right onto the B3247. After 5 miles (8km), in Crafthole, turn right signed to Portwrinkle. Distance: 7 miles (11¼km).

⑮ Portwrinkle.

Not much remains of this once-flourishing fishing village, but it's a quiet spot for a leg stretch, with lovely (if slightly exposed) beaches. There are 19th-century coastguard cottages at the west end, and a boathouse used by customs on the lookout for smugglers in the 17–18th centuries. No shop or pub, but there is the Whitsand Bay Hotel. ⏱ *15 min.*

Retrace your route to the B3247 and turn right, signposted Cawsand. After 5 miles (8km) pass Tregantle Fort; turn right signed to Whitsand. Turn right on the single track lane by the entrance to Polhawn Fort; at the T-junction, turn right. Pass Rame Church to reach Rame Head. Distance: 7 miles (11¼km).

⑯ Rame Head.

The farther east you travel, the more English and less Cornish the surroundings feel; pre-1844, the Rame Peninsula was part of England, and many local names stem from Old English, not Cornish. Rame Head has vestigial Iron Age fortifications and great views; St Germanus Church, consecrated in the 13th century, has graves of shipwrecked mariners. ⏱ *15 min.*

Retrace your route past the church and keep ahead; at the T-junction, turn right (to Kingsand/Cawsand) and aim for Cawsand car park. Distance: 1¼ miles (2km).

⑰ Cawsand & Kingsand.

Allow time to explore the narrow alleyways and brightly painted cottages of these two atmospheric old fishing villages. Both have a strong tradition of smuggling, encouraged by a ready market in Plymouth. The old Devon–Cornwall border runs between them, marked by a small stream: there are pubs, cafés and two safe, sandy beaches. ⏱ *1 hr.*

Travel Tip

Don't try to drive into the villages: leave your car in the car park and walk.

From the car park, turn right; at the junction, turn right onto the B3247 signed to Mount Edgcumbe. Distance: 3½ miles (5½km).

18 Mount Edgcumbe. See p 62.

Retrace your route along the B3247; through Millbrook pick up the signs for Torpoint. Pass Tregantle Fort and turn right signed to Anthony. At the junction with the A374, turn right signposted Torpoint (brown signs). Distance: 8½ miles (13¾km).

19 Antony House & Woodland Garden. The elegant home of the Carew Pole family dates from the early 18th century and is one of Cornwall's finest classical mansions and now a NI property. The gardens were landscaped by Humphry Repton and include a formal garden with topiary, a knot garden and the National Collection of daylilies. The woodland garden (not NT) has rhododendrons, magnolias, camellias and azaleas. ⏱ *4 hr. Antony, Torpoint PL11 2QA.* ☎ *01752 812191. www.nationaltrust.org.uk. Adult £6.30, child £3.15, family (2 adults) £15.75, family (1 adult) £9.50. NT members free (including Woodland Garden on days when house is open). House: Apr–May & Sept–Oct Tues–Thurs 1–5pm, plus Suns in Jun–Aug. Woodland garden: £5.45, 1 Mar–31 Oct 11am–5:30pm.*

Turn right onto the A374 signed to Liskeard. After 7 miles (11¼km), in Polbathic turn right signposted St Germans. Pass through the village to meet the A38; turn right (to Plymouth). After 3½ miles (5½km), turn left (to Callington); at the A388, turn left (to Launceston). At Viverdon Down roundabout, turn right (brown signs) and follow the signs to Cotehele. Distance: 19¾ miles (31¼km).

20 Cotehele. See p 63.

Return to the A388 and turn right (to Callington). At the roundabout, turn left onto the A390 (to Liskeard). Distance: 8 miles (13km).

Calstock & the River Tamar

Cotehele's gardens cascade to the River Tamar. A gentle walk of around 1½ miles (2½km) leads from Cotehele Quay upstream to the picturesque village of **21 Calstock,** beneath the 117ft (36m), 12-arch viaduct, built 1904–08 to carry the railway line to Bere Alston. Silver, lead, copper and arsenic were mined in the valley between the 14th and 19th centuries, and soft fruit and vegetables (grown on the valley's sheltered slopes) were exported from the quaysides. The walk passes the Chapel in the Wood—built by Sir Richard Edgcumbe in 1490 in gratitude for his escape from his enemies near here in 1483—and a little pottery in Danescombe Valley.

The Roseland Peninsula & the Lizard

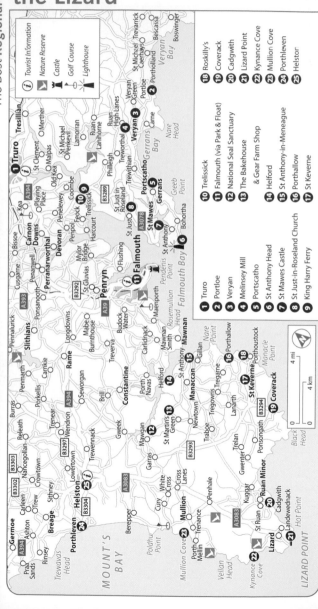

Legend:

- *i* Tourist Information
- Nature Reserve
- Castle
- Golf Course
- Lighthouse

1. Truro
2. Portloe
3. Veryan
4. Melinsey Mill
5. Portscatho
6. St Anthony Head
7. St Mawes Castle
8. St Just-in-Roseland Church
9. King Harry Ferry
10. Trelissick
11. Falmouth (via Park & Float)
12. National Seal Sanctuary
13. The Bakehouse & Gear Farm Shop
14. Helford
15. St Anthony-in-Meneague
16. Porthallow
17. St Keverne
18. Roskilly's
19. Coverack
20. Cadgwith
21. Lizard Point
22. Kynance Cove
23. Mullion Cove
24. Porthleven
25. Helston

Mid-south Cornwall's alluring peninsulas have a distinctive flavour. The Lizard culminates in the British mainland's most southerly point and the less-visited Roseland, east of the Carrick Roads, has tranquil creeks, ancient churches and well-to-do villages. The Lizard's east coast is similar, but the central area is flat and open, with the underlying serpentine rocks supporting the beautiful Cornish heath that flowers in late summer and is unique to this area.

START: Truro. Trip Distance: **148½ miles (239km). Trip Length: 3 days. Maps: OS Explorers 103, 105.**

❶ Truro. *See p 137.*

Follow the signs to the A390 St Austell. After 5½ miles (8¾km), turn right onto the A3078 to St Mawes. Just under 5 miles (8km) later by a garage, turn left to Portloe; follow the signs (the car park is on the right). Distance: 11½ miles (18½km).

One of Veryan's five round houses.

❷ Portloe. This quaint fishing village huddles in a deep rocky inlet. The 17th-century Lugger Hotel (a former smuggler's haunt, now a smart and stylish place) stands by the slipway, where fishing boats are hauled to the quay. ⏱ *30 min.*

Continue through the village, uphill; at the staggered crossroads, keep ahead to Veryan. Distance: 2¾ miles (4½km).

❸ Veryan. Five cob (a traditional Cornish building material mixture of

earth, sand, straw and water) roundhouses scattered throughout the village were built c. 1820 by the vicar (Rev Jeremiah Trist). The circular design was intended to prevent

Melinsey Mill.

St Mawes and St Mawes Castle.

the Devil from hiding in corners. The church of St Symphorian has Britain's longest grave, occupied by 19 crew of the German barque *Hera*, shipwrecked in 1914. ⏱ *30 min. Village shop, New Inn, café at Elerkey Art Gallery.*

Turn left (a pub is on the left), and then right (to St Mawes). Melinsey Mill is on right at the bottom of the hill. Distance: ¾ mile (1¼km).

4 Melinsey Mill. This 16th-century watermill, one of the smallest in Cornwall, has been restored to working order. A café is inside where local crafts are on sale and there's a 'magic trail' around a tranquil millpond. ⏱ *1½ hr. Veryan, nr Truro TR2 5PX.* ☎ *01872 501049. Free admission. Daily Apr–end Oct 10am–5:30pm; closed Mon in Apr, May & Oct. Evening meals Jun–Aug; phone for details.*

Turn right. At the junction, turn left onto the A3078 to St Mawes; after 2 miles (3¼km), turn left (to Portscatho); just under 1 mile (1½km) later, turn left; car park is on the right. Distance: 3¾ miles (6km).

5 Portscatho. This historic pilchard-fishing port is popular with families for its safe sandy beaches,

galleries, gift shops and the Plume of Feathers pub. ⏱ *30 min.*

Continue through the village; at the T-junction in Gerrans, turn left to St Anthony. After about 2½ miles (4km), turn left as signed to St Anthony Head. Distance: 3¾ miles (6km).

6 St Anthony Head. Ros means promontory in Cornish (hence the name Roseland). St Anthony Head's southern extremity has splendid views of the Carrick Roads. *See p 102. Free admission to Promontory.*

Retrace your route to Gerrans; just beyond the village, turn left; on meeting the A3078, turn left (to St Mawes). Follow car park signs to the harbour. Distance: 8¾ miles (14km).

7 St Mawes Castle. *See p 58.*

Continue past the castle; bear left onto the A3078 to St Just in Roseland; turn left for the church. Distance: 2½ miles (4km).

8 St Just-in-Roseland Church. Sloping steeply to St Just Creek, this picture-postcard churchyard billows with luxuriant subtropical vegetation. It's a popular film and TV location. Joseph of Arimathea

St Justus-in-Roseland's Church.

King Harry Ferry.

is said to have landed here en route for Glastonbury. ⏱ *1 hr.*

Return to the A3078; turn left, immediately left for the King Harry Ferry. Distance: 3¼ miles (5¼km).

⑨ King Harry Ferry. The chain ferry links Roseland with the west bank of the Fal. The service has been operating since 1889; the present ferry (the seventh) was launched in May 2006. ⏱ *5 min. Feock, Truro TR3 6QJ.* ☎ *01872 862312. www.kingharryscornwall. co.uk. Ferry crossing: single (car) £4.50, return £7.50. Ferries depart every 20 min (summer) from 7:20am (9am Sun/Bank Hol) until 21:20pm.*

Celtic cross at St Justus-in-Roseland's Church.

Travel Tip

Using the King Harry Ferry saves a 27-mile (43½km) road journey.

Keep ahead; Trelissick is on left. Distance: ½ mile (¾km).

⑩ Trelissick. *See p 28.*

Turn left; after 2 miles (3¼km), turn right at the T-junction; turn left onto the A39 (to Falmouth). At the double mini roundabout (at Treluswell), turn left on the B3293 (to Penryn); at the Ponsharden roundabout, keep ahead (to Falmouth), and almost immediately turn left into the Park and Float. Distance: 9 miles (14½km).

⑪ Falmouth (via Park & Float). *See p 101.*

Turn right; take the left at the roundabout (A39 to Truro). After 2½ miles (4km), turn left onto the A394 to Helston. After 2½ miles (4km), turn left to Gweek. In the village turn right, immediately left (brown signs). Distance: 10¼ miles (16½km).

⑫ National Seal Sanctuary. *See p 37.* Retrace your route to the centre; turn left over two bridges. Turn left up the Gweek creek (St Keverne); at the roundabout, turn left (to Mawgan). After just under 2 miles (3¼km), the farm shop is on the right. Distance: 4 miles (6½km).

⑬ The Bakehouse & Gear Farm Shop. Locally produced vegetables, bread, cakes, pizzas, pies and

Coverack harbour.

organic Cornish pasties are sold here, as well as fresh fish (except after stormy weather). *Café. Mawgan, Helston TR12 6DE.* ☎ *01326 221150. Daily 9:30am–4:30pm (except Sun).*

Turn right through St Martin/Newtown; turn left to Helford. After just over 2 miles (3¼km), turn left: car park is on the right at the bottom of the hill. Distance: 4¾ miles (7½km).

🕙 **Helford.** Once a haunt of smugglers, this village now contains mostly holiday homes. Daphne du Maurier's novel Frenchman's Creek (p 107) is a romantic tale of pirates who haunted these waters during the Napoleonic Wars. Stop at either The Shipwright's Arms or Down by the Riverside Café. 🕙 *1½ hr.*

Travel Tip

Don't drive into Helford: there's no parking or turning. A passenger ferry runs to Helford Passage.

Retrace your route to the first junction; turn left to St Anthony (single-track lane). Distance: 2 miles (3¼km).

🕤 **St Anthony-in-Meneague.** This village is little more than a tiny boatyard and a 12th-century church. Gillan Creek is magical, especially at high tide. A small shop is open in summer. 🕙 *45 min.*

Continue up Gillan Creek. At head, turn left (to Porthallow). After just under 2 miles (3¼km), turn left (single track lane); turn left into village. Distance: 3¾ miles (6km).

🕤 **Porthallow.** This quiet, unspoilt fishing village has a good pub (The Five Pilchards), a shop and an art gallery. The sheltered beach is popular with families. 🕙 *15 min.*

Continue along the lane, eventually to St Keverne. Distance: 2¼ miles (3½km).

🕤 **St Keverne.** The 15th-century church of St Akeveranus has a distinctive octagonal spire, probably built as a daymark (navigation aid for shipping): 400 shipwreck victims lie in the churchyard. There are two pubs and the Greenhouse Organic Restaurant overlooking the square. Leaders of the Cornish Rebellion of 1497 and the Prayer Book Rebellion of 1549 hailed from here. 🕙 *30 min.*

From the square, turn left and almost immediately right past the

Coverack.

Cadgwith.

school. At the crossroads, turn right. Distance: 1 mile (1½km).

⓲ Roskilly's. Essential visiting for ice cream fans (p 41). ⏱ *2 hr. Tregellast Barton, St Keverne, Helston TR12 6NX.* ☎ *01326 280479. www.roskillys.co.uk. Daily summer 10am–6pm/9pm and winter weekends.*

Turn right; at the B3294, turn left (to Coverack). Distance: 2 miles (3¼km).

⓳ Coverack. Popular with holidaymakers and retired folk, Coverack has two safe beaches and an attractive harbour. thewave@coverack (café) and the Paris Hotel (named after a local shipwreck) are by the harbour. ⏱ *30 min.*

Continue past the harbour; bear sharp right before hotel. After just less than 2 miles (3¼km), turn right at the T-junction (to Helston). At the B3293 at Zoar, turn left; after 1¾ miles/2¾km) turn left (to Cadgwith). Turn right in Kuggar; at the crossroads, keep ahead (to St Ruan); just under 1 mile (1½km) later turn sharp left between posts to car park. Distance: 9 miles (14½km).

⓴ Cadgwith. This pretty village still has an active fishing fleet. The Old Cellars Restaurant occupies a former pilchard cellar (1782) and Cadgwith Cove Inn dates back 300 years. ⏱ *45 min.*

Retrace your route through the posts; turn left (to Lizard). After 1 mile (1½km), turn left for the Grade Church; or keep ahead to the A3083. Turn left for Lizard; pass through the village to the Lizard Point car park. Distance: 4 miles (6½km).

㉑ Lizard Point. The Lizard's curious mottled rocks date back 400 million years; buy a piece of worked serpentine. You can have tea in the

Mullion Cove.

Poldhu Cove.

Polpear or Wavecrest cafés; bird-watchers should look out for choughs (p 36). **The Lizard Light-house Heritage Centre** (www.lizardlighthouse.co.uk) was commissioned in 1752 and the lighthouse is open to the public. ⏲ *1½ hr. Parking free for NT members. April Sat–Wed 12–4pm; May Sat–Wed 11am–4pm; June Sat–Wed 11am–5pm; July daily 11am–6pm; Aug daily 11am–7pm; Sept Sat–Wed 11am–5pm; Oct Sat–Wed 11am–4pm; Nov and Dec Sun–Wed 11am–4pm; adult £4, children (under 12) £3, concessions £3.50, family £10; with lighthouse tour £5/2.50/4.50/12.50.*

Travel Tip

The UK mainland's most southerly point is far less spoiled than Lands End, but still gets very crowded in summer.

Blue Anchor sign, Helston.

Retrace your route through the village, soon turning left into the NT car park. Distance: 2 miles (3¼km).

㉒ Kynance Cove. You get picture-postcard scenery here: rugged cliffs, white sands and turquoise sea (plus a café!). ⏲ *30 min. Parking free for NT members.*

Retrace your route to the A3083; turn left. After under 4 miles (6½km) later, turn left (towards Mullion Cove). Follow the road through Mullion; turn left as signposted. Distance: 6¾ miles (11km).

㉓ Mullion Cove. The picturesque harbour, completed in 1895, has an old pilchard cellar and net store, and there's a lifeboat station that was operational 1867–1909; in the six years to 1873 there were nine shipwrecks here. Porthmellin Café overlooks the harbour. ⏲ *30 min.*

Retrace your route to Mullion; at the end of the one-way system, turn left past Poldhu Cove. At the A3083, turn left (to Helston). Pass RNAS Culdrose; at the round-about turn left onto the A394 (to Penzance). Pick up the signs to Porthleven; at the double mini roundabout, turn left onto the B3304. Distance: 11¾ miles (19km).

㉔ Porthleven. This is England's most southerly port, a bustling fish-ing village with many galleries and workshops, and once famed for shipbuilding. The harbour was con-structed in 1825 to provide a safe haven for shipping on a notoriously dangerous stretch of ocean coast-line. The Ship Inn, its oldest pub, is said to be haunted. 🕐 *45 min.*

Continue to the A394; turn right (to Helston). At the double mini roundabout, turn left (for car parks). Distance: 3½ miles (5½km).

Coronation Park, Helston.

Canon outside the Guildhall, Helston.

㉕ Helston. This ancient stannary town with fine old buildings is best known for its spring festival. Flora Day and the Furry Dance involve flowers, a mummers' (folk) play (Hal-an-Tow) and formal dancing in the streets all day. The Blue Anchor Inn brews Spingo ale. Outside the Guildhall is a cannon rescued from HMS Anson, wrecked on Loe Bar in 1807. Coronation Park has a boat-ing lake, café, playgrounds and ducks. 🕐 *1½ hr.*

Turn right at the mini roundabout onto the A394 towards Falmouth; after 10 miles (16km) at Treliever roundabout, turn left onto the A39 (towards Truro). At the roundabout on the edge of Truro, turn right (onto the A39); turn left for the town centre. Distance: 35 miles (56¼km).

The **Isles of Scilly**

1. Tourist Information Centre
2. Boatmen's Association kiosk
3. St Mary's Bike Hire
4. Bike Shed
5. Island Rover
6. Longstone Heritage Centre
7. Carreg Dhu Community Garden
8. The Isles of Scilly Museum
9. The Isles of Scilly Wildlife Trust
10. The Sailing Centre, Porthmellon
11. The Boat Shed
12. Dibble & Grub, Porthcressa
13. Juliet's Garden Restaurant, Porthloo
14. Tresco Abbey Gardens
15. Gallery Tresco, New Grimsby
16. Tresco Stores
17. The New Inn, New Grimsby
18. The Island Hotel, Old Grimsby
19. St Martin's Diving School
20. White Island
21. Glenmoor Cottage Gift Shop
22. Churchtown Farm
23. Polreath Guest House, Higher Town
24. St Martin's Bakery, Moo Green
25. The Seven Stones
26. St Martin's on the Isle Hotel
27. Little Arthur's Wholefood Café & Bistro, Higher Town
28. Beady Pool
29. The Bulb Shop
30. St Agnes Boating
31. The Turk's Head, Porth Conger
32. Troytown Farm
33. Coastguards Café
34. Hell Bay
35. Bryher Boat Services
36. Fraggle Rock Bar-Café
37. Vine Farm Café
38. Hell Bay Hotel

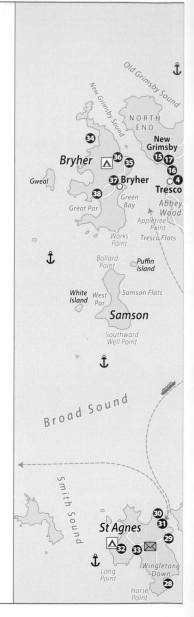

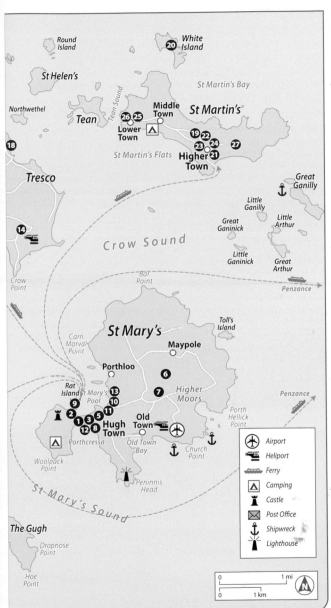

Round Island
St Helen's
Northwethel
Tean
Tean Sound
White Island
20
St Martin's Bay
Middle Town
26 25
Lower Town
St Martin's
St Martin's Flats
19 22
23 24
21
27
Higher Town
18
Tresco
14
Crow Point
Great Ganilly
Little Ganilly
Great Ganinick
Little Arthur
Crow Sound
Little Ganinick
Great Arthur
Bar Point
Penzance
Carn Morval Point
St Mary's
Toll's Island
Maypole
Porthloo
6
7
Higher Moors
Penzance
Rat Island
St Mary's Pool
9
13
10
2 1 3 5 11
12 8
Hugh Town
Porthcressa
Old Town
Old Town Bay
Church Point
Porth Hellick Point
Penzance
Woolpack Point
Peninnis Head
St Mary's Sound

The Gugh
Dropnose Point
Hoe Point

Symbol	Legend
✈	Airport
🚁	Heliport
⛴	Ferry
⛺	Camping
♜	Castle
✉	Post Office
⚓	Shipwreck
🔆	Lighthouse

0   1 mi
0   1 km
N

Call them the Isles of Scilly or just Scilly (but not the Scilly Isles and never the Scillies). England's smallest AONB (Area of Outstanding Natural Beauty) lies sprinkled in the Atlantic 28 miles (45km) southwest of Lands End. Although well offshore, Scilly is an administrative part of Cornwall and easily accessible by boat, helicopter or plane from the mainland. Boats run regularly from the main island, St Mary's, radiating to all the other inhabited islands, which you can explore in any order. START: **Penzance. Trip Length: Optional. Map: OS Explorer 101.**

Most people who visit the magical Isles of Scilly, even if only for a single day, resolve to return for a longer stay. This low-lying granite archipelago is part of the same huge mass of rock that forms Dartmoor in Devon, and the Cornish moorland around Bodmin and West Penwith. There are five inhabited islands—six if you count the one house (empty for most of the time) on Gugh, which is joined to St Agnes at low water. In addition, more than 150 uninhabited islands, shape-shifting with each tide, lie scattered across the shallow turquoise seas. Fringed with beaches of soft, pale sand, the archipelago has the exotic appeal of some faraway holiday paradise, an impression enhanced by the balmy, frost-free climate and colourful sub-tropical plants.

In winter, fierce storms sometimes batter the islands, and gales blow uninterrupted across the Atlantic (no land deflects the force of wind or waves between Scilly and the east coast of North America). At times the weather is too rough for the helicopter service or the inter-island boats to operate, but generally Scilly is renowned for its mild winters, and hot summer sunshine.

The islands are also famous for their exceptional range of flora and fauna: plants usually encountered in much more exotic locations thrive here, and flowers grown commercially on Scilly (mainly narcissi) bloom months ahead of the mainland. Scilly's offshore location at the extreme edge of the UK provides first landfall for a huge variety of migrating birds, drawing many

Town Beach, Hugh Town, St Mary's.

'twitchers' (keen birdwatchers) here in spring and autumn, armed with high-tech optics and cameras at the ready.

Legend has it that the islands were once part of the Lost Land of Lyonesse (a sort of Arthurian Atlantis), but archaeological evidence reveals that the islands have been continuously inhabited since the Bronze Age, around 4,000 years ago.

The **❶ Tourist Information Centre** in Hugh Town on St Mary's is a mine of information about Scilly, including accommodation (☎ 01720 422536; www.simplyscilly.co.uk). But if you plan to stay on the islands, book well ahead: Scilly is a popular holiday choice and its limited accommodation is over-subscribed for much of the year.

Getting There

Travelling to the Isles of Scilly is not cheap. The fastest, most convenient, and perhaps most memorable way to get there is to take a helicopter from Penzance (☎ 01736 363871; www.islesofscillyhelicopters.com). Regular flights go to St Mary's and (less frequently) to Tresco (journey time about 20 minutes). Skybus flies small planes to Scilly from St Just near Lands End and several other UK airports in the southwest year round (☎ 0845 7105555; www.ios-travel. co.uk); an aerial view of the islands on a clear day is unforgettable. Subsidised transfer buses run from Penzance mainline station to the airfield if you arrive by train. It's cheaper (but slower) to sail from Penzance on the *Scillonian III*, a ferry service operating from late March to early November, taking around 2½ hr (contact details as for Skybus).

Getting Around by Boat

Some visitors choose to travel no farther than the main island, St Mary's. But if you're staying on Scilly

Scillonian III at St Mary's quay.

for longer than a day, take a trip to one or more of the 'out islands'. The inter-island boat service is very efficient. Launches leave Hugh Town on St Mary's at around 10am and 2pm daily, returning at lunchtime and late afternoon. There are special trips to watch seals and puffins, visit uninhabited islands and sail round the UK's farthest-flung lighthouse, the Bishop Rock. Tickets for all trips can be purchased at the **❷ Boatmen's Association kiosk** on the quay (☎ 01720 423999; www.scillyboating.co.uk). The out islands all operate their own boat services, and run specific trips on certain days. Note that there's no transport to or from the islands on Sundays.

Getting Around on Land

Non-residents aren't allowed to take vehicles to the islands. Bike hire is available both on St Mary's (**❸ St Mary's Bike Hire** ☎ 01720 422289) and Tresco (**❹ Bike Shed** ☎ 01720 422849; www.tresco. co.uk); the other islands are small enough to explore on foot. St Mary's has only 9 miles (14½km) of surfaced road; you're more likely to encounter tractors on the out islands. On St Mary's the **5 Island Rover** (☎ 01720 422131; www.islandrover.co.uk) (an open-top bus service) runs at least twice a day in summer and takes just over an hour (ideal for a quick overview if you're on a day trip).

St Mary's

The largest island in the group (measuring 2½ miles x 1¾ miles (4 x 2¾km) has a population of just over 1,500. St Mary's is the hub of the islands' transport system and has the only town on Scilly, Hugh Town, which lies between two sandy beaches: Town and Porthcressa. The quayside bustles with activity all day long, but it's easy to escape the crowds and explore the rest of the island via 30 miles (48km) of nature trails and coastal paths. Secluded sandy beaches, Bronze Age burial chambers, rocky promontories and a smattering of beautifully located cafés ensure plenty of diversions en route. More active souls can play golf on the nine-hole course, try kayaking, sailing, windsurfing or cycling, and go bird-watching or flower-spotting.

Don't miss: **6 Longstone Heritage Centre** at Holy Vale where you can learn all about the history of and contemporary life on the islands (☎ 01720 4237770); **7 Carreg Dhu Community Garden,** in the heart of St Mary's (☎ 01720 422404); **8 The Isles of Scilly Museum,** Church Street (☎ 01720 422337); **9 The Isles of Scilly Wildlife Trust** on the Quay (☎ 01720 422153; www.ios-wildlifetrust.org.uk); **10 The Sailing Centre** at Porthmellon (and also on Tresco) (☎ 01720 422060; www.sailingscilly.com); and for eating out **11 The Boat Shed** (☎ 01720 423881; www.the-boat shed.co.uk); **12 Dibble & Grub** at Porthcressa (☎ 01720 423719); and **13 Juliet's Garden Restaurant** at Porthloo (☎ 01720 422845; www.julietsgardenrestaurant.co.uk), with wonderful views over the water to Hugh Town.

Tresco

Like the other Isles of Scilly, Tresco is owned by the Duchy of Cornwall, but unlike the others, it has been leased to the Dorrien-Smith family since 1834, and has the feel of a private estate. Tresco measures about 2 x 1 mile (3¼ x 1½km), and has a

New Grimsby quay, Tresco.

population of around 150. It has one of Scilly's most luxurious hotels, the Island, set on a private beach on the sheltered northwest coast, and a recent holiday development at New Grimsby (The Flying Boat Club). Protected from full force of the prevailing winds by the neighbouring island of Bryher, Tresco's climate is exceptionally mild, as indicated by the famous Abbey Gardens. The north of the island is the wildest and most rugged part; the rest is gentler, with fine sandy beaches.

Don't miss: **14 Tresco Abbey Gardens** (p 30); **15 Gallery Tresco** at New Grimsby (☎ 01720 424925); **16 Tresco Stores** near Farm Beach (an uber-trendy delicatessen) (☎ 01720 422806); and for eating out **17 The New Inn** at New Grimsby (☎ 01720 422844) and **18 The Island Hotel,** Old Grimsby (☎ 01720 422883). www.tresco.co.uk.

St Martin's

The next-largest island is St Martin's, to the northeast of Tresco. St Martin's is a 2-mile (3¼km) ridge of granite, with a rugged north coast and a stunning beach at Great Bay on the northeast coast. The western side (protected by Tresco) is where you'll find the small hamlets of Lower, Middle and Higher Town

Tresco Abbey Gardens.

containing a resident population of just over 100. There's a sheltered campsite here surrounded by low walls and hedges of escallonia. The only surfaced lane links the two quays at Lower and Higher Town; boats use different landing stages depending on the state of the tide. Par Beach at Higher Town quay is one of the best.

Don't miss: **19 St Martin's Diving School** (also on St Mary's) (☎ 01720 422848; www.scillydiving.com); a walk (only possible at low tide) onto **20 White Island** on the island's northeast tip; **21 Glenmoor Cottage Gift Shop** near the bakery; or **22 Churchtown Farm** for flowers (☎ 01720 422169; www.scillyflowers.co.uk). For eating

Gig Racing

Scilly is internationally famous for its gig-racing championships held annually in May. Gigs are traditional 32ft (9¾m) six-oared wooden working boats dating from the 19th century. In those days competing pilot crews would row out from the islands to assist ships as they sailed into these shallow, hazardous waters. You can watch the island gig crews practising: the women's teams go out on Wednesday evenings, and the men's on Friday evenings. Boats for spectators usually leave St Mary's quay at 7:45pm.

The Turk's Head, St Agnes.

out, try **㉓ Polreath Guest House,** Higher Town (☎ 01720 422046; www.polreath.com); **㉔ St Martin's Bakery,** Moo Green (☎ 01720 423444); **㉕ The Seven Stones** pub (☎ 01720 423560); **㉖ St Martin's on the Isle Hotel** (bistro) (☎ 01720 422090; www.stmartinshotel.co.uk); or **㉗ Little Arthur's Wholefood Café & Bistro** (and vineyard) at Higher Town (☎ 01720 422457; www.littlearthur.co.uk).

St Agnes

Lying across the deep-water channel of St Mary's Sound, St Agnes is the most southerly of Scilly's inhabited islands; it's also the UK's most southerly outpost. The only island without a hotel, St Agnes is particularly appealing if you're searching for the simple life or trying to get away from it all—as soon you step ashore your worries just melt away. The island measures just 1 mile (1½km) across, has a population of around 90, and you can walk around it in about an hour. **㉘ Beady Pool** on the southern arm is the site of a 17-century shipwreck (samples of its cargo of beads are still occasionally found here). The Big Pool on the northern side provides the first fresh water for migrant birds crossing the Atlantic, and is a magnet for birdwatchers.

Don't miss: **㉙ The Bulb Shop**—take some Scilly bulbs home with you (☎ 01720 423002; www.stagnes flowers.co.uk); **㉚ St Agnes Boating** for a trip to see seals on the Western Rocks (☎ 01720 422704; www.st-agnes-boating.co.uk); and for eating out **㉛ The Turk's Head,** Porth Conger (☎ 01720 422434), **㉜ Troytown Farm,** homemade ice cream (☎ 01720 423713; www.troytown.co.uk); and **㉝ Coastguards Café** (☎ 01720 422197; www.coastguardscafe.co.uk). www.st-agnes-scilly.org.

Bryher

Covering only 327 acres (133 hectares), with a resident population of just 80, Bryher is the smallest and most westerly of Scilly's inhabited islands. It receives the full force of the Atlantic storms; Hell Bay on its exposed and rocky west coast is well named. Bryher's rugged wildness resembles St Agnes rather than its more 'managed' neighbour Tresco (you can wade between Bryher and Tresco at very low tides). Bryher means 'place of hills' in Celtic, and Watch Hill gives one of the best views in Scilly. The southern and eastern shores are peaceful and sheltered, and Rushy Bay on the island's southernmost point is especially beautiful.

Don't miss: a visit to **㉞ Hell Bay** in stormy weather; **㉟ Bryher Boat Services** (☎ 01720 422886); **㊱ Fraggle Rock Bar-Café,** Scilly's smallest pub (☎ 01720 422222); and for eating out **㊲ Vine Farm Café** (☎ 01720 422260). **㊳** The **Hell Bay Hotel** is part of the Tresco Estate (☎ 01720 422947; www.tresco.co.uk/stay/hell-bay). www.bryher-ios.co.uk. ●

The
Savvy Traveller

Before You Go

Tourist Information

The Tourist Information Centre in the nearest town generally has the most up-to-date information on the local area (see Chapter 5).

Bodmin Shire Hall, Mount Folly, Bodmin PL31 2DQ; ☎ 01208 76616; email: bodmintic@visit.org.uk; www.bodminlive.co.uk.

Boscastle The Harbour, Boscastle PL35 0HD; ☎ 01840 250010; email: boscastlevc@btconnect.com; www.visitboscastleandtintagel.com.

Bude TIC and Canal Visitor Centre The Crescent Car Park, Bude EX23 8LE; ☎ 01288 354240; email: budetic@visitbude.info; www.visitbude.info.

Camelford (seasonal) **North Cornwall Museum,** The Cleese, Camelford PL32 9PL; ☎ 01840 212954; email: manager@camelfordtic.eclipse.co.uk.

Falmouth 11 Market Strand, Prince of Wales Pier, Falmouth TR11 3DF; ☎ 01326 312300; email: info@falmouthtic.co.uk; www.discoverfalmouth.co.uk.

Fowey 5 South Street, Fowey PL23 1AR; ☎ 01726 833616; email: info@fowey.co.uk; www.fowey.co.uk.

Hayle (seasonal) Hayle Library, Commercial Road, Hayle TR27 1RR; ☎ 01736 754399; email: hayle.library@cornwall.gov.uk.

Helston Customer Services Office, Isaac House, Tyacke Road, Helston TR13 8RR; ☎ 01209 614000 (Mon–Fri only).

Isles of Scilly Hugh Street, Hughtown, St Mary's TR21 0LL; ☎ 01720 424031; email: tic@scilly.gov.uk; www.simplyscilly.co.uk.

Launceston Market House Arcade, Market Street, Launceston PL15 8EP; ☎ 01566 772321; email:

Previous page: Cape Cornwall.

Launcestontic@btconnect.com; www.visitlaunceston.co.uk.

Liskeard Foresters Hall, Pike Street, Liskeard PL14 3JE; ☎ 01579 349148; email: tourism@liskeard.gov.uk; www.liskeard.gov.uk.

Looe (seasonal) The Guildhall, Fore Street, East Looe PL13 1AA; ☎ 01503 262072; email: looetic@btconnect.com.

Lostwithiel Lostwithiel Community Centre, Liddicoat Road, Lostwithiel PL22 0HE; ☎ 01208 872207; email: tourism@lostwithieltic@wanadoo.co.uk; www.lostwithieltic.org.uk.

Mevagissey St Georges Square, Mevagissey PL26 6UB; ☎ 01726 844440; email: info@mevagissey-cornwall.co.uk; www.mevagissey-cornwall.co.uk.

Newquay Marcus Hill, Newquay, Cornwall TR7 1BD; ☎ 01637 854020; email: newquay.tic@cornwall.gov.uk; www.visitnewquay.org.

Padstow Wadebridge, Rock and Polzeath, Red Brick Building, North Quay, Padstow PL28 8AF; ☎ 01841 533449; email: padstowtic@btconnect.com; www.padstowlive.com.

Penzance Station Approach, Penzance TR18 2NF; ☎ 01736 362207; email: 01736 363600; www.visiit-westcornwall.com.

Perranporth 8 Tywarnhayle Square, Perranporth TR6 0ER; ☎ 01872 575254; email: 01872 572971; www.perranporthinfo.co.uk.

Redruth (seasonal) The Cornwall Centre, Alma Place, Redruth TR15 2AT; ☎ 01209 219048; email: cornishstudieslibrary@cornwall.gov.uk; www.cornwall.gov.uk/cornwallcentre.

St Agnes 5 Churchtown, St Agnes TR5 0QW; ☎ 01872 554150; email: ticstagnes@yahoo.co.uk; www.st-agnes.com.

St Austell By Pass Service Station, Southbourne Road, St Austell PL25 4RS; ☎ 01726 879500; tic@cornish-riviera.co.uk; www.cornish-riviera.co.uk

St Ives The Guildhall, Street an Pol, St Ives TR26 2DS; ☎ 01736 796297; email: ivtic@penwith.gov.uk; www.visit-westcornwall.com.

St Just The Library, Market Street, St Just, Penzance TR19 7HX; ☎ 01736 788165; email: stjusttourist@cornwall.gov.uk; www.visit-westcornwall.com.

St Mawes The Roseland Visitor Centre, The Millennium Rooms, The Square, St Mawes; TR2 5AG ☎ 01326 270440; email: manager@roselandinfo.com; www.stmawesandtheroseland.co.uk.

Tintagel Bossiney Road, Tintagel PL34 0AJ; ☎ 01840 779084; email: tintagelvc@btconnect.com; www.visitboscastleandtintagel.com.

Truro Municipal Buildings, Boscawen Street, Truro TR1 2NE; ☎ 01872 274555; email: tic@truro.gov.uk www.truro.gov.uk.

Useful Websites
www.visitcornwall.co.uk
www.cornwall-online.co.uk
www.chycor.co.uk

Southeast Cornwall:
www.visit-southeastcornwall.co.uk
www.secta.org.uk
www.bestofsecornwall.co.uk

Bodmin Moor:
www.bodminmoor.co.uk
www.visitbodminmoor.co.uk

North Coast:
www.north-cornwall.com
www.thisisnorthcornwall.co.uk

Mid-Cornwall (excluding north coast):
www.kingharryscornwall.co.uk
www.acornishriver.co.uk
www.thelizard.co.uk

Southwest Cornwall:
www.westpenwith.com
www.visit-westcornwall.com

www.go-cornwall.com
www.landsendarea.co.uk

Isles of Scilly:
www.simplyscilly.co.uk
www.scillyonline.co.uk

VISA information
Entry visas are not required for stays of less than 3 months by anyone holding a passport from European Union countries, Switzerland, some Commonwealth countries including Australia, Canada and New Zealand and some non-European countries including Japan and the USA. Check the website of the UK Border Agency, www.ukvisas.gov.uk, well in advance of your visit.

The Best Time to Go
Cornwall is a popular destination for both short breaks and longer holidays. If the weather is set fair, many people make last-minute plans. Book ahead to be sure of your chosen accommodation between March and October, especially on the Isles of Scilly.

Trains and hotels fill up quickly, and during the summer holidays you need to book campsites and caravan parks too. For quiet getaways, come outside the major holiday periods; choose the winter months, when accommodation is cheaper (many places close out of season, of course). Christmas and New Year are popular times to visit.

Public Holidays
England has eight public holidays, when banks, most offices and some shops are closed. Don't expect many shops in Cornwall (except in tourist towns) to be open on Sundays. New Year's Day: 1 January; Good Friday: March/April; Easter Monday: March/April; Early May Bank Holiday: 1st Monday in May; Spring Bank Holiday: last Monday in May;

Summer Bank Holiday: last Monday in August; Christmas Day: 25 December; Boxing Day: 26 December.

The Weather

Cornwall has the mildest weather in the UK. The maritime location moderates winter temperatures so that frost and snow are rare, whereas summer temperatures are higher than expected at this latitude (on a par with some Mediterranean resorts). The mean maximum summer temperature is around 66°F (19°C), but can rise to the 80°Fs (high 20°Cs). Sunshine hours reach around 1500 hours per year, about 7 hours a day in the summer months. Rain falls all year, brought by weather fronts from the Atlantic, but tends to be more frequent in winter when prevailing southwesterly winds can reach gale force. Cornwall's weather is unpredictable: it can start sunny in the south and be raining by lunchtime, with the reverse a few miles away on the north coast!

The Isles of Scilly have their own microclimate: winter temperatures are even milder than in mainland Cornwall (average January temperature is 50°F/10°C), and summers hotter and hours of sunshine greater (around 25% more per month than London). Scilly suffers Atlantic storms in winter. www. destinationcornwall.co.uk has webcam and live weather reports; www. cornwalls.co.uk/weather links into Met Office reports; www.bbc.co.uk/ cornwall and www.metoffice.gov.uk give local forecasts.

Mobile Phones

Mobile (cell) phone coverage is generally good, but you won't get a signal in some of the more sheltered valleys. UK sim cards can be bought at mobile phone shops in the bigger towns and some supermarkets. They cost £6–10 and can be topped up with prepaid vouchers. The UK's international dialling code is ☎ 0044.

Getting **There** & Getting **Around**

By Car

Driving to Cornwall is the most popular choice for most holidaymakers. Apart from the 250,000 or so who spend extended holidays here, around 5 million people visit the county for short trips, most during the summer. The M5 is the main route into Cornwall, leading from Birmingham via Bristol to Exeter, where it splits into the A30 (via Bodmin to Penzance) and the A38 (via Plymouth to Bodmin, to meet the A30). In 2007, a long stretch of A30 in mid-Cornwall was upgraded to dual carriageway, but a section farther west is single carriageway and gets heavily congested. Off the main

routes, roads can be narrow with few places to overtake. Beware of high hedges, non-motorised traffic (cyclists, walkers, animals) and hold-ups (local and farm traffic); keep cool, use your map and adjust travelling times.

By Rail

First Great Western (☎ 08457 000125; www.firstgreatwestern. co.uk) and Cross Country Trains (☎ 0844 811 0124; www.cross countrytrains.co.uk) run services from the rest of the UK. Direct main line services run from London Paddington, Waterloo, Bristol and

Birmingham; London Paddington to Penzance takes around 5 hours. Car rental is available at mainline stations (www.europcar.com, www.hertz.co.uk and local providers). Scenic branch-line services run to Falmouth, St Ives, Newquay, the Looe Valley and the Tamar Valley (www.carfreedaysout.com).

For details and tickets contact National Rail Enquiries (☎ 08457 484950; www.nationalrail.co.uk) or The Trainline (on-line booking service, www.thetrainline.com).

By Air

Formerly run with support from RAF St Mawgan, Newquay Airport received the go-ahead to run as a civilian service in late 2008, and has full commercial international airport status. Visitors to southeast Cornwall may prefer to fly into Plymouth—Air Southwest—in south Devon.

Air Southwest ☎ 0870 241 8202; www.airsouthwest.com: Cork, Bristol, Dublin, Glasgow, Leeds Bradford, London City, London Gatwick, Manchester, Newcastle, Plymouth and via Plymouth: Jersey, Guernsey.

BmiBaby ☎ 0871 224 0224; www.bmibaby.com: Birmingham, Durham Tees Valley.

Flybe ☎ 0871 700 2000; www.flybe.com: Aberdeen, Belfast, Birmingham, Bristol, Cardiff, Doncaster, Dublin, Edinburgh, Exeter, Glasgow, Guernsey, Jersey, Leeds Bradford, Livepool, London Gatwick, Manchester, Newcastle, Norwich, Southampton.

Jet2 ☎ 0871 226 1737; www.jet2.com: Belfast, Blackpool. Edinburgh, Leeds Bradford, Manchester, Newcastle.

For flights to the Isles of Scilly, p 164.

By Bus

National Express (☎ 08705 808080; www.nationalexpress.com) runs coaches between major towns across the UK. Contact Tourist Information Centres for local bus information, or visit Traveline (☎ 0871 2002233; www.traveline.org.uk).

Fast **Facts**

BANKING HOURS Normally Mon–Sat 9:30am–3:30pm (variations in smaller towns).

BIKE RENTALS *See p 85.*

BUSINESS HOURS Shops usually open Mon–Sat 9am–5pm. In tourist hotspots they may remain open later, and on Sun.

CASH MACHINES (ATMS) Found in main towns, villages, petrol stations and some shops and hotels.

CREDIT CARDS Visa and Mastercard accepted in most outlets; American Express, Diners Club and EuroCard accepted at some major establishments.

DOCTORS *See hospitals p 174.*

ELECTRICITY 240 volts, 50Hz, 13-amp, three-pin, rectangular plugs are used; adapters are easy to find.

EMBASSIES Full details of embassies in the UK are on the Foreign and Commonwealth Office website www.fco.gov.uk.

Australia Australian High Commission, Australia House, Strand, London WC2B 4LA; ☎ 020 7379 4334.

Canada Canadian High Commission, MacDonald House, 1 Grosvenor Square, London W1K 4AB; ☎ 020 7258 6600.

USA 24 Grosvenor Square, London W1A 1AE; ☎ 020 7499 9000.

EMERGENCY ASSISTANCE Police, Ambulance, Fire or other Emergency ☎ 999.

GAY & LESBIAN TRAVELLERS Homosexuality is legal in the UK; the age of consent for men and women is 16. www.stonewall.org.uk, www.queery.org.uk, www.tht.org.uk.

HOSPITALS See www.nhs.uk for hospitals and doctors (GPs).

Bodmin Hospital ☎ 01208 251300.

Camborne Redruth Community Hospital ☎ 01209 881688.

Falmouth Hospital ☎ 01326 434700.

Fowey District Hospital ☎ 01726 832241.

Royal Cornwall Hospital Truro ☎ 01872 250000.

St Austell Community Hospital ☎ 01726 291120.

Most towns have health centres and doctors' surgeries. Check with your hotel, tourist information or telephone directory for details. Or see www.nhs.uk or call NHS direct on 0845 4647 for health advice and information.

INSURANCE Always travel with adequate insurance cover. If you plan high-risk activities such as climbing or watersports, make sure that your policy covers them. EU citizens should travel with a European Health Insurance Card (EHIC), which entitles you to free or reduced state medical treatment if you need emergency care while in the UK.

INTERNET ACCESS/CAFÉS Some of the major town have Internet cafés; also try public libraries. Many hotels and B&Bs have Internet access and WiFi.

MAIL & POSTAGE Post offices are in most main towns and some villages; see www.postoffice.co.uk and click on branch finder, or ☎ 08457 223344. Post offices are generally open Mon–Fri 9am–5:30pm, Sat 9am–12:30pm. Some bigger branches have longer opening hours, and smaller branches shorter.

MONEY & EXCHANGE BUREAUX Sterling is the UK's currency. One pound is divided into 100 pence. Notes come in denominations of £5, £10, £20 and £50; there are 1p, 2p, 5p, 10p, 20p, 50p, £1 and £2 coins. Most major banks will exchange foreign currency.

PARKING Many town car parks are operated by local councils and you need to buy a ticket. On-street parking may be restricted to residents. If you're in violation of the regulations you might get a parking fine (much more costly than the cost of a parking ticket), or even worse, have your vehicle clamped or towed away.

In the countryside, parking rates vary depending on who operates them. If you have a National Trust membership card, you can park free of charge in some areas (p 8).

PHARMACIES Chemists are open during normal shopping hours, and operate on a rota system for emergencies at other times (a notice on the door should indicate the timetable). Alternatively, ask at your hotel or contact NHS direct ☎ 0845 4647, www.nhs.uk/servicedirectories/Pages/ServiceSearch.aspx.

SAFETY Cornwall has a relatively low crime rate. Visitors should take the usual precautions with valuables and personal safety.

SENIOR TRAVELLERS Cornwall is a popular destination for all ages; anyone over 60 is entitled to discounts at many attractions and museums.

SHOPPING For farmers markets, below. Details of other markets are given in Best Towns, p 101–140.

SMOKING Smoking is now illegal in all enclosed public areas in the UK, including buses and trains, bars, restaurants, shops, banks and entertainment establishments except in smoking-designated areas.

STAYING HEALTHY Standards of health and hygiene are high in the UK. However, during summer visitors should take care against the sun, which can be deceptively hot (even when overcast). Wear a suitable high-factor sunscreen when outside. A sun hat is advisable; if travelling with children be aware that they need extra protection (especially babies). Drink plenty of water to replace lost fluids.

TELEPHONES Public phones are located all around Cornwall, though many don't accept coins, only phonecards.

TIME The UK is on Greenwich Mean Time (GMT) in winter and British Summer Time (1 hour ahead) between the last Sunday in March and last Sunday in October. The UK is 5 hours ahead of US Eastern Standard Time. For a time check ☎ 123.

TIPPING Gratuities should be in the region of 10%, but check whether service is already included on your bill.

TRAVELLERS WITH DISABILITIES If you have a disability or specific needs contact Disability Information before you travel: ☎ 01332 295551, minicom ☎ 01332 295581, www. disabilityinformation.com. If you require any assistance at the airport, notify your airline when you book your ticket.

USEFUL PHONE NUMBERS The cheapest number for **Directory Enquiries** is ☎ 118 226, followed by 118 390, 118 848, 118 500 and 118 118. Or look online for free www.bt.com and www.yell.com for business numbers.

VAT Current rate of VAT is 17.5%. Food (except in restaurants or takeaways), books and newspapers, children's clothes and shoes, and public transport are zero-rated.

WATER Tap water is safe to drink. Many brands of local and imported still and sparkling bottled waters are available, cheapest in larger supermarkets.

Cornish **Farmers' Markets**

Callington 2nd and 4th Fri 9am–1pm
Carnon Downs last Sat 9am–12pm
Coads Green 4th Sat
    9:30am–12:30pm
Falmouth Tues 9am–2pm
Grampound Produce 4th Sat
    10am–1pm
Grampound Road 3rd Sat
    9am–12:30pm
Helston 1st Sat 9:30am–1pm
Ladock 1st Sat 9am–12pm
Launceston Butter 1st Sat 9am–1pm
Launceston Fri 9:30am–2:30pm
Lostwithiel 2nd Fri 10am–3pm
Mevagissey Sun 10am–2pm

Pendeen 1st and 3rd Sat 10am–1pm
Pensilva 2nd Sat 9:30–12:30pm
Penzance Fri 9am–3pm
Redruth Fri 9am–3pm
Rilla Mill 3rd Sat 9am–12pm
St Erth Sat 10am–12pm
St Ives Thurs 9:30am–4pm
St Marys (Isles of Scilly) 1st Sat
    9am–12pm
St Neot Sat 9am–12pm
Stithians 3rd Sat 10am–12pm
Stoke Climsland 1st Sat
    9am–12:30pm
Truro Sat 9am–4pm and Wed
    8:30am–4pm

Index

Photo **Credits**